DRAWINGS OF THE NORTH AMERICAN INDIANS

GEORGE CATLIN

DRAWINGS OF THE NORTH AMERICAN INDIANS

WITH AN INTRODUCTION BY
PETER H. HASSRICK

DOUBLEDAY & COMPANY, INC.
GARDEN CITY, NEW YORK
1984

DESIGNED BY LAURENCE ALEXANDER

Library of Congress Cataloging in Publication Data

Catlin, George, 1796–1872
Drawings of the North American Indians.

1. Catlin, George, 1796-1872. 2. Indians of North
America — Pictorial works. 3. West (U.S.) in art.
I. Title. NC139.C37A4 1984 741.973
ISBN: 0-385-19119-7
Library of Congress Catalog Card Number 83-45238
Copyright © 1984 by Hirschl & Adler Galleries, Inc.

FOREWORD

George Catlin pursued the depiction of the American Indian with an intense single-mindedness of purpose. The extensive literature on this artist's life has recorded the facts of his endeavor and has interpreted its motivations in much detail. In this facsimile volume, a rare opportunity is fulfilled to bring the public into direct communication — in words as well as in pictures — with the artist himself.

It is fundamental to the artistic process that it have as one of its objectives the reaching of a constituency. Like the tree that falls unobserved in the forest, the artist's unseen product lacks the dimension of sensory experience. By his choice of subject matter and the method of its execution and exposure, the artist seeks to inform his audience of his view of the quality of life. Catlin's efforts in this regard encompassed a complex combination of social and political factors. Without oversimplifying, it would be reasonable to say that these efforts had as their goal the presentation of a set of facts about the diverse appearance of American Indians at the middle of the nineteenth century and the achievement of an understanding that their existence as it had been observed was in jeopardy.

With the benefit of hindsight, the drastic reality of Catlin's perceptions is made clear. The final two drawings, showing *Wi-jun-jon*, son of the Chief of the Assiniboin tribe, before and after a visit to Washington, add a vivid satirical coda to the work. This somewhat shocking ending is in stark contrast to the steady, restrained procession of images which precedes it. In all it is apparent that Catlin sought in his work an understanding among men through education and uplift of the spirit. We are all the more fortunate that in so doing he produced artistic works of surpassing quality.

Although Catlin was a fine artist, dedicated to his personal vision, his efforts to sustain a market for his work were unsuccessful. The poignancy with which he renders in pencil and describes in the accompanying texts the 215 subjects in this Souvenir Album is heightened by reading his letter of 1859 to the Duke of Portland in which, with the most delicate language, he asks the sum of £75 for his work, emphasizing the value by suggesting that he "could not afford to *repeat* such a labour for a less price than £175."

In the same letter, Catlin reveals that the Souvenir Albums were created by him "with a view of publishing in that form, but which plan I have abandoned." One hundred and twenty-five years later, Hirschl & Adler Galleries has joined with Doubleday to realize the

V

artist's wish. Of the ten known Souvenir Albums, all but the one used in the production of this book are in permanent museum or library collections, and are available for viewing, if at all, on a necessarily limited basis. It is thus a special pleasure to have had the opportunity of accomplishing George Catlin's original objective to make these extraordinary drawings available to the widest possible audience.

Stuart P. Feld
Robert D. Schonfeld

One hundred and fifty years ago, the artist and celebrated man of American science, George Catlin, left his home in New York City to travel among the Indian tribes west of the Mississippi. Compelled by a desire to create a pictorial record of Indian culture before the disappearance of these native American people and their way of life, Catlin began his journey in 1830. Within a decade he had completed over 500 paintings of the American West, depicting Indian life and customs with a genuine respect and profound understanding unprecedented in his century. Assembled as *Catlin's Indian Gallery,* the collection toured American and European capitals for the next dozen years and, in replica form, for an additional twenty. In 1879, seven years after Catlin's death, the Smithsonian Institution acquired the artist's original collection, thus fulfilling one of his lifelong dreams.

Under sponsorship of the Smithsonian, an Idaho lawyer named Thomas Donaldson completed an exhaustive treatise on the collection in 1885, revealing the magnitude of Catlin's contribution as the first artist to make a serious study of the western tribes. Donaldson's recognition of Catlin's accomplishments led to a systematic reappraisal of Indian culture which was initiated by the Eleventh Census of the United States in 1890. With Donaldson's encouragement, five younger-generation American painters — Peter Moran, Julian Scott, Walter Shirlaw, Gilbert Gaul, and Henry R. Poore — were assigned to the census to provide pictorial documentation. The census artists discovered, of course, that much had changed since the time of Catlin's forays on the western prairies some sixty years before. For whereas Catlin had been witness to the opening of the frontier, Peter Moran and his colleagues arrived to view its demise. In heeding Donaldson's urgings, Americans acknowledged both the importance of artistic documentation in general and the fundamental role which Catlin had played in preserving the image of native Americans before the dynamics of the evolving Anglo frontier created a pervasive and often devastating transformation.

Being a man of remarkable drive, unbounding hubris, and uneven skills as a writer and painter, Catlin presented a controversial figure in his own time. He was praised and maligned by some of the greatest men of the nineteenth century. Many of his fellow artists, including Alfred Jacob Miller and Rudolph Friederich Kurz, considered him a charlatan.[1] Yet others praised him highly. In the late 1860s, while Catlin languished poverty-stricken and neglected in Brussels, his contemporary, the art critic Henry Tuckerman, shed summary light on a waning career.

> Here [in Catlin's Gallery] was a result of art, not drawn merely from academic practice or the lonely vigils of a studio, but gathered amid the freedom of nature. Here were trophies as eloquent of adventure as of skill, environed with the most national associations, and memorials of a race fast dwindling from the earth. With what interest would after-generations look upon these portraits, and how attractive to European eyes would be such authentic "counterfeit present-ments" of a savage people, about whose history romance and traditions alike throw their spells! To visit the scenes whence Catlin drew these unique specimens of art, to study the picturesque forms, costumes, attitudes, and grouping of Nature's own children; to share the grateful repast of the hunter, and taste the wild excitement of frontier life, in the very heart of the noblest scenery of the land, was a prospect calculated to stir the blood of one with the true sense of the beautiful, and a natural relish for woodcraft and sporting.[2]

Catlin died in 1872, a bitter and disregarded veteran of American science and art. In the intervening years, however, he has perhaps had more influence on those artists and ethnologists whose vision has been directed beyond the Mississippi than any other single person.

As the ice began to clear from the Missouri in the spring of 1830, a slender, dark-haired man in his mid-thirties, bearing the marks of a tomahawk wound on his left cheek, made his appearance in the burgeoning frontier community of St. Louis. He was armed with two important tools for fulfilling his dream in the Far West. One was his supply of artists' implements—brushes, paints, and canvas—and the other, an impressive letter of introduction from the Secretary of War to the distinguished territorial governor of Missouri, General William Clark. The letter of introduction would bring with it the key to America's western gateway, and his paints would bring him fame.

Catlin was born in 1796 of a well-educated rural Pennsylvania family. His father, because of poor health, retired from a legal career early in life to become a farmer. The young Catlin thus grew up with nature, acquiring a sustained adoration for it. The Catlin farm was in the Susquehanna Valley, a well-traveled route to the West. It was there that George first learned from travelers about the mysterious expanses beyond the relatively tame frontier of his home ground. His schooling at an academy in Wilkes-Barre opened his mind to the disciplines of history, geography, natural philosophy, English, and the classics. Together the two experiences combined to provide Catlin with requisite formal powers of observation mixed with a romantic quest for adventure.

At the insistence of his father, George studied law in Litchfield, Connecticut, and, after completing a fourteen-month course, passed the state bar examination. Returning to Pennsylvania, he practiced law with modest success for the next several years. His heart, however, was not absorbed in jurisprudence but rather with a new and consuming urge to paint.

By 1821 Catlin had turned his back on his law career and had gained considerable notice as a local painter of portraits and ivory miniatures. At age twenty-seven he moved to Philadelphia, where he gained admission for exhibition of his works in the Pennsylvania Academy of the Fine Arts—no mean accomplishment for a self-trained artist.

In the world of art as well as science, Philadelphia provided an ample store of mentors. Charles Wilson Peale's Museum gathered the best of both these worlds. Its contents and conceptual philosophy offered a guidepost for bright and thirsty minds like that of George Catlin. Yet there were other models as well. The style of his early work in some instances suggests that Catlin may have been indebted to Philadelphia's distinguished Thomas Sully. The general ambiance of the city also afforded inspiration and spiritual motivation, which ushered Catlin through a critical learning phase. He emerged confident and ready to capture a larger and more sophisticated audience in New York City. This became his next challenge and the state's governor, DeWitt Clinton, his most celebrated patron. It seemed as though Catlin were on his way to a life of painting social worthies and political dignitaries, but two things went awry. First the New York critics offered harsh assessments of his work. The noted savant William Dunlap, for example, claimed that Catlin, with his portrait of Governor Clinton, had "the distinguished notoriety of having produced the worst full-length which the city of New-York possesses."[3] Second Catlin longed for life and inspiration outside the parlor and studio. As he later recounted, my mind was continually reaching for some branch or enterprise of the art, on which to devote a whole life-time of enthusiasm; when a delegation of some ten or fifteen noble and dignified-looking Indians, from the wilds of the "Far West," suddenly arrived in the city, arrayed and equipped in all their classic beauty...exactly for the painter's palette![4]

Catlin's penchants for adventure, for the quest of classical beauty, for assisting in the search to broaden knowledge about the world around him, and for painting were sated by a newly awakened ambition to be an artist among the Indians. His younger brother, Julius, shared his enthusiasm for a western trip to collect portraits and artifacts sufficient to return east and establish a museum. Julius' untimely death in 1828 provided the stimulus for Catlin's first trip west two years later and the initial fulfillment of his life's ambition. The dream was summarized by Catlin himself, who stated that he had set out with the "determination of reaching, ultimately, every tribe of Indians on the Continent of North America...I designed, also, to procure their costumes, and a complete collection of their manufactures and weapons, and to perpetuate them in a *Gallery unique,* for the use and instruction of future ages."[5]

Hence, at great expense and sacrifice to himself and his bride Clara, whom he had married in 1828, Catlin departed for the West in 1830. He went first to St. Louis, the common site of embarkation for travelers into the trans-Mississippi frontier. His first two years of work were in relatively tame environs. He traveled with government officials to nearby Indian villages. One of his most productive sojourns was in the company of General Clark to Fort Crawford, near the junction of the Mississippi and Wisconsin rivers, in the summer of 1830. The portraits painted there were of Indian leaders, many of whose tribes had sent representatives to Washington in years past. They were already familiar with the White Man. In the fall he spent time among the Delaware, Kickapoo, Potawatomi, and Shawnee, who under government coercion had moved west across the Mississippi. They were already civilized, to one degree or another, a circumstance which pointed to the urgency of Catlin's task. Time was essential as he strove to acquaint himself with the western Indians before President Andrew Jackson's Indian Removal Act of 1830 went into full effect, forcing cultures indigenous to the eastern woodlands onto western lands. Not only did Catlin fear acculturation but also the inevitable demise of the Plains Indians themselves. "The buffalo's doom is sealed," he wrote,

> and with their extinction must assuredly sink into real despair and starvation, the inhabitants of these vast plains, which afford for the Indians, no other possible means of subsistence; and they must at last fall a prey to wolves and buzzards, who will have not other bones to pick.[6]

After an eastern respite of over a year, Catlin returned to St. Louis late in 1831. His primary purpose seems to have been to prepare for his next summer's journey up the Missouri. However, he was able to complete several portraits of a small Indian delegation on its way through St. Louis to Washington. *Wi-jun-jon,* a distinguished Assiniboin warrior (plate 171), was one who sat for Catlin in St. Louis that year. Catlin described the encounter of artist and Indian.

> *Wi-jun-jon* was the first, who reluctantly yielded to the solicitations of the Indian agent and myself, and appeared as sullen as death in my painting room — with eyes fixed like those of a statue, upon me, though his pride had plumed and tinted him in all the freshness and brilliancy of an Indian's toilet. In his nature's uncowering pride he stood a perfect model; but superstition had hung a lingering curve upon his lip, and pride had stiffened it into contempt.[7]

Through *Wi-jun-jon,* Catlin's mission was clearly defined. In the spring of 1832, when the artist prepared to board the newly built steamboat *Yellowstone* for her maiden voyage from St. Louis to Fort Union, *Wi-jun-jon* was there. After returning from Washington, he and his companions were on their way back to their homes on the upper Missouri. Catlin noticed, however, that a major transformation had occurred. "*Wi-jun-jon* made his appearance on deck, in a full suit of regimentals! He had in Washington exchanged his beautifully garnished and classic costume, for a full-dress 'en militaire'."[8] (Plates 214 and 215.)

Catlin's 4,000-mile odyssey took him to the mouth of the Yellowstone River, offering him exposure to most of the Northern Plains tribes. When he returned to St. Louis in October of that year, he proudly boasted nearly 170 paintings (many of them, needless to say, still little more than sketches) of Missouri landscapes and Indian portraits.[9] He could also for the first time articulate the special feeling he had developed for his entrancing subject.

My enthusiastic admiration of man in the honest and elegant simplicity of nature, has always fed the warmest feelings of my bosom, and shut half the avenues to my heart against the specious refinements of the accomplished world. This feeling, together with the desire to study my art, independently of the embarrassments which the ridiculous fashions of civilized society have thrown in its way, has led me to the wilderness for a while, as the true school of the arts.[10]

The West for Catlin was the premiere studio, its natural element a symbol of national promise and arcadian retreat. "The wilderness of our country," he observed, "afforded models equal to those [from] which the Grecian sculptors transferred to the marble such inimitable grace and beauty."[11]

When Catlin returned east late in 1832, he undertook the completion of the paintings which were conceived in the field, and he began his search for an audience. Cincinnati and Pittsburgh provided his initial targets. To his pleasant surprise, his collection of paintings and ethnological specimens were well received. This brief show tour had proven that there was a popular demand for such material.

To further his learning and broaden the dimensions of his collection, he traveled west again in 1834. This time he sought new scenery and faces among the native people of the Southern Plains. In the company of Colonel Henry Dodge's Dragoons, Catlin ventured onto the grassy prairies of present-day Oklahoma, the home of the great horsemen of the plains — the Comanche. Although illness weakened and depleted the expedition's ranks, and Catlin himself suffered greatly, the trip proved well worth the effort, providing a welcome new chapter to Catlin's growing narrative of adventure and many important new portraits to his burgeoning collection of art.

The year 1835 found Catlin on the upper Mississippi, where he painted St. Anthony Falls and portraits of Indians around Fort Snelling. On his way back downriver, he painted the great Sauk and Fox chief Keokuk (plate 134), whose image had already been made famous by several other painters of the day.

By now Catlin was prepared in his mind to return to civilization and, through a scheduled tour of his painting collection, to reap some remunerative rewards for the long years of travel and preparation. The beginning of a tour, however, was postponed by one of Catlin's rather impulsive moves—a trip to the pipestone quarries west of Fort Snelling in the summer of 1836. By the following spring, though, his show was open in Albany, and his sights were set on New York City.

Catlin was somewhat apprehensive about New York City. He had, back in 1834, written that the wilds were his inspiration and that big cities were sources of restraint and confinement. "I have learned more of the essential parts of the art in the three last years, than I could have learned in New-York in a life time."[12] But now he had to test those skills against a New York audience.

The New York *Morning Herald* for September 25, 1837, announced the artist's arrival in that city with the following notice:

> CATLIN'S INDIAN GALLERY opens for exhibition this evening the 25th inst. in the Lecture Room of Clinton Hall, and will be continued each evening during the week. There will be several hundred portraits exhibited, as well as splendid specimens of costume, paintings of their villages, dances, buffalo hunts, religious ceremonies, etc. collected by himself amongst the wildest tribes in America during an absence from this city of seven years. Mr. Catlin will be present at all of these exhibitions, giving illustrations and explanations in the form of a lecture, and it is desirable that all visitors will be in and seated at half past 7, that they may be able to see the whole collection.

Within a week, Catlin's apprehension had changed to a feeling of a dream fulfilled. The *Morning Herald* for October 3 recognized the popularity of his production in which the public was apprised, through visual means and the artist's lecture, of the American Indian's complexity and remarkable cultural contribution. In his lectures Catlin strove to celebrate both the noble and human nature of his wilderness brethren. He did so "nightly to delighted audiences, who listen to the strange traditions, manners and customs, of the tribes he has visited, illustrated by hundreds of paintings, with breathless attention." Catlin was soon forced to find a larger hall for his show.

By the time of the New York opening, the *Catlin's Indian Gallery* collection comprised almost 500 works. He had already begun to think of a permanent home for his paintings, although his short-term goals were to circulate the collection to enthusiastic crowds in Philadelphia, Boston, and Washington. Feeling that the latter city, the nation's capital, would make an ideal resting place for the *Indian Gallery,* Catlin moved his collection there directly from New York. There he planned to persuade appropriate political interests that a national museum might be founded with his *Indian Gallery* as its foundation. In fact, according to Catlin's biographer, Harold McCracken, a resolution had already been introduced in the House of Representatives and referred to the Committee of Indian Affairs, that would have approved the purchase of Catlin's collection by the government.[13] The matter was never resolved, however, because the session (1837–38) was too near closing at the time of its introduction.

The exhibition nonetheless opened in Washington in the spring of 1838, and Catlin was confident that the nation's capital, once exposed to his wilderness marvels, would be more favorably inclined. Spending heavily on advertising and promotion, the artist was able to win over some influential partisans to his cause, including Henry Clay and Daniel Webster. But Washington did not supply the audience Catlin had wished and, recognizing the financial exigencies of keeping his show on the road and public perception positive, he continued on his way, opening in Baltimore in early July of that year.

Catlin's aspiration to see his collection become the core of a national museum remained undiminished throughout his remaining life. He would return the idea to the doorstep of Congress many times in subsequent years. Yet for the time being, once his East Coast tour was completed and his initial salvos to Congress had come to naught, he decided to focus his sights on Europe. His intentions were to attract a new audience and, through international exposure, to solidify his chances on the home front for positive consideration by Washington. With this in mind, he departed for England in late autumn of 1839. The New York *Evening Star* bid Catlin farewell with a telling allusion to the fate of his museum idea.

> Catlin's Indian Gallery...will be closed after the lapse of a single week and will never again be exhibited in America...It is one of the most remarkable and interesting works that the genius and labor of an individual has created in this age and country...Nothing could redound more to the patriotism, national pride, and honor of our country, than the purchase by Congress of this collection of Aboriginal Curiosities, to enrich a National Museum at Washington.[14]

"After having made an exhibition of my Indian Collection for a short time, in the United States," wrote Catlin, "I crossed the Atlantic with it—not with the fear of losing my scalp, which I sometimes entertained, when entering the Indian wilderness."[15] Catlin's intentions were clearly educational. Even the English government allowed him and his vast collection of materials to enter the kingdom free of normal duties. His own discussions of the enterprise reveal that he was guided by a genuine pedagogical mandate.

> I was launched upon the wide ocean, with eight tons freight, consisting of 600 portraits and other paintings which I had made in my sojourn of eight years in the prairies and Rocky Mountains of America — several thousands of Indian articles, costumes, weapons, etc., with all of which I intended to convey to the English people an accurate account of the appearance and condition of the North American tribes of Indians.[16]

The task was such that Catlin had even retained a curator, Daniel Kavanagh, to assist him in the care and presentation of the *Indian Gallery.* On February 3, 1840, the London *Times* alerted its readership that Mr. Catlin's *Indian Gallery* collection would soon be open to the public. It would, they contended, be of special interest to "the antiquary, the naturalist, and the philosopher." London's Egyptian Hall was his new showplace, and so successful were the performances that Catlin negotiated for a three-year lease.

For the edification of his London audience, Catlin published *A Descriptive Catalogue of Catlin's Indian Gallery.* This volume listed 507 paintings, along with his collection of artifacts referred to by the artist as "Indian curiosities and manufactures." In the introduction of this catalogue, Catlin called on recognized authorities such as William Clark and Henry Schoolcraft to offer testimonials about the authenticity of the scenes and portraits, their "fidelity and correctness." As for their artistic merit, Catlin offered a modest apology. "The world will surely be kind and indulgent enough to receive and estimate them, as they have been intended, as *true and fac-simile traces of individual and historical facts;* and forgive me for their present unfinished and unstudied condition, as works of art." The London *Times* had not mentioned connoisseurs of art among those who would find the Catlin display revealing. The reviewer excused the paintings as not being "in the finished style of modern art" but remarkable in their "vigor and fidelity of outline which arises from the painter having beheld what he transmits to canvas."[17] Thus they observed that much of the artistic value of Catlin's work derived not from aesthetic underpinnings but from the inherent vitality of execution.

Vigor of presentation was also important to Catlin's early successes in England. In New York and other American cities, he had often dressed himself as an Indian to assist in the effective preservation of mood during his lectures. Now he hired a group of men and women to perform as Indians. The London *Times* for April 19, 1841, described this innovative addition to Catlin's program.

> After detailing a variety of...interesting and instructive matters, for which the limits of this notice are wholly insufficient, Mr. Catlin proceeds to exhibit a series of *tableaux vivans,* by 20 living figures arrayed in beautiful Indian costumes, fully armed and equipped, illustrative of the warlike habits as well as the domestic customs of the portion of the human family. These *tableaux* are arranged with most picturesque and thrilling effects.

Real Indians were later arranged for through outside contacts. Longing for financial success while he continued to await a favorable decision from Congress, Catlin turned more and more toward dependence on showmanship. The instructive, educational, and artistic implications of his *Indian Gallery* received increasingly less of his attention and energy as he focused on creating an extravaganza of near Wild West show proportions. He presented a troupe of Ojibwa Indians before Queen Victoria in 1844 (Buffalo Bill would later perform for her Golden Jubilee in 1887), and he was subsequently persuaded to take on the management of a group of Iowa Indians, an enterprise which eventually drained his energies, patience, and resources. His wife admonished him in later years that such activities were counterproductive and antithetical to his initial philosophical goals of being an artist and spokesman for the Indians.

There were many frustrations involved in trying to keep the *Indian Gallery* exhibit running. One of the largest problems resulted from the enthusiasm stirred within the local community of artists for Catlin's images. He and his curator, Daniel, were constantly troubled with "efforts by artists and amateurs to make copies in the room for paintings and design."[18] Catlin resented this intrusion into the exclusivity of his imagery and eventually posted a large sign which stated, *"No copying is allowed in the rooms."*[19] On several occasions Daniel almost came to blows in defense of this regulation.

During his early years in England, Catlin proudly accomplished two major publishing ventures. In 1841 he printed at his own expense a major two-volume treatise on his travels and observations. Entitled *Letters and Notes on the Manners, Customs, and Condition of the North American Indians,* this profusely illustrated book was already in its fourth printing by 1844. Of the many books Catlin would author in subsequent years, *Letters and Notes* is by far the most substantial production. Though fanciful in some details, especially regarding the artist's travels, it was then (and is still today) the definitive published document on Plains Indian ethnology. When it was first issued, the *Westminster Review* lauded it with twelve pages of notice.

> This is a remarkable book, written by an extraordinary man. A work valuable in the highest degree for its novel and curious information about one of the most neglected and least understood branches of the human family. Mr. Catlin, without pretension to talent in authorship, has yet produced a book which will live as a record when the efforts of men of much higher genius have been forgotten.[20]

The book, despite its success, did not bring Catlin riches. As a result, he embarked in 1844 on the production of a set of twenty-five chromolithographs incorporating some of the more popular images from the *Indian Gallery. Catlin's North American Indian Portfolio* contains examples of Catlin's artistic expression which some scholars have felt exceed the originals in excellence.[21]

When neither of these publishing ventures produced the kind of financial return Catlin had hoped to attract, the artist and his collection left England for greener pastures in France. He exhibited in Paris from the summer of 1845 until early the next year. King Louis Philippe even provided a gallery in the Louvre for the artist's collection and entertained, and was entertained by, the troupe of Indians then accompanying Catlin. Commissions, such as a set of fifteen paintings of Indians for Louis Philippe completed in 1846, helped to offset the artist's losses incurred when several of the Indians contracted smallpox.

He continued his efforts, from abroad, to persuade Congress of their need to acquire his collection. In hopes of seeing a national gallery established, a group of American artists working in Europe wrote supportively of U.S. government purchase of Catlin's collection. In a letter transmitted to the Senate, they wrote:

Interesting to our countrymen generally, it is absolutely necessary to American artists. The Italian, who wishes to portray the history of Rome, finds remnants of her sons in the Vatican; the French artist can study the ancient Gauls in the museums of the Louvre; and the Tower of London is rich in the armour and weapons of the Saxon race.

Your memorialists, therefore, most respectfully trust that Mr. Catlin's collection may be purchased and cherished by the federal government, as a nucleus for a national museum, where American artists may freely study the bold race who once held possession of our country, and who are so fast disappearing before the tide of civilization.[22]

Signing this plea from Paris were such fellow American artists as John Vanderlyn, Thomas Rossiter, and John F. Kensett. Some of this support was no doubt generated by the enlightened self-interest of these artists.

Catlin, however, had his critics among the artist community as well. Alfred Jacob Miller, who had been to the Rocky Mountains in 1837 with Captain William Drummond Stewart, saw Catlin in London in 1842. He was unimpressed, writing home that Catlin was thought of as something of a "humbug."[23] Rudolph Friederich Kurz, an artist inspired by Catlin's contemporary, Karl Bodmer, painted on the upper Missouri in the late 1840s and early 1850s. In his diary for September 17, 1851, Kurz stated that Catlin was regarded as a humbug on the frontier as well. He was especially perplexed by Catlin's propensity for "distorting narratives for the sake of effect." Though he found the ethnographic and anthropologic detail to be essentially correct in Catlin's book, "the drawings...are for the most part in bad taste, and to a high degree inexact..."[24]

Despite these and other disparaging remarks from artists who knew the West of Catlin's acquaintance, his first decade in Europe seems to have been quite positive and well-received. So confident was he of his contribution to the world's art and learning that in 1848 he had published a sequel to *Letters and Notes,* which he titled *Eight Years' Travels and Residence in Europe.* Though interesting, this latter work was far less substantive, providing little more than anecdotes of an American in Europe.

When Catlin returned from Paris to London, following the deposal of Louis Philippe in 1848, his gallery had grown to over 600 works.

Unfortunately, the additional paintings were not enough to garner renewed enthusiasm for the collection. Catlin encountered increasing difficulty in attracting new audiences and made a series of poor personal financial investments, as a combined result of which he found himself seriously in debt. One reason for his difficulties may have been the rising competition. In 1850 the *Bulletin of the American Art-Union* listed as showing in London alone no less than three panorama exhibitions of American subjects (including one called "Fremont's Diorama," showing the overland route to California) and seven of other subjects, ranging from the Queen's visit in Ireland to one of Tête Noir Pass in Switzerland featuring a "torrent of real water."[25]

Beginning in 1846, a Joint Committee on the Library recommended once again that Congress purchase Catlin's collection. By then, "with the Regents of the Smithsonian Institution having, by resolution, agreed to give this collection a place and to preserve it in their Gallery of Art,"[26] a second report was called for. Not until 1853 was a bill introduced to this effect. It passed the House of Representatives but failed by one vote in the Senate.

Fortunately for Catlin, when he had first come to England, he had been properly presented to a wide variety of distinguished and well-connected people. An Englishman, Charles A. Murray, who had been with Catlin for some time in the West, was Master of the Queen's Household. As Catlin recalled, his

> friend Mr. Murray was constantly present, and introduced me to very many of them, who had the kindness to leave their addresses and invite me to their noble mansions, where I soon appreciated the elegance, the true hospitality and refinement of English life.[27]

Some of these acquaintances matured into friendships which were sustained over the years. And some of these friends provided a market for Catlin in the late 1840s, when he began formally to reproduce replicas from the original *Indian Gallery* collection for sale. It was at this time also that he first produced sets of bound volumes of drawings which he called "Albums Unique."[28] Since there is rarely anything unique about these albums, and since they are generally described on the title pages as a "Souvenir of the North American Indians...," we will refer to them as "Souvenir Albums." The Duke of Portland's portfolio is one of about ten known to have been produced in the decade following his exit from France.

Many of the Souvenir Albums were purchased by noted families. Catlin must have viewed such sales as a better alternative than placing his collection permanently in Europe, still hoping his option in America would pan out. For example, before leaving London for Paris he had been offered £7,000 for the *Indian Gallery* collection by an English lord but declined, refusing to see the collection hidden away in some musty castle.[29] Even as late as 1870, when corresponding with the New-York Historical Society regarding its possible interest in his work, he mentioned his resistance to the thought of his collection being in "the perpetual imprisonment of a nobleman's mansion."[30] Sets of drawings and commissioned works, whether duplicating subjects in the *Indian Gallery* or consisting of new material, were another matter.

The forerunner to the Souvenir Albums appears to have been an 1849 album commissioned by or sold to Sir Thomas Phillipps, one of England's most celebrated bibliophiles. Belonging today to the Thomas Gilcrease Institute of American History and Art in Tulsa, Oklahoma, the album consists of fifty drawings heightened with watercolor. Its title page reads, "Souvenir of the North American Indians as They Were in the Middle of the Nineteenth Century," and many of the scenes are derived directly from elements in the original collection. New compositions were also introduced which became standard subjects for later Souvenir Albums and what would be known as his "Cartoon Collection,"[31]—a set of paintings in oil produced to replace the *Indian Gallery* exhibit, which Catlin had lost in 1852 due to financial reverses.

The Duke of Portland's Souvenir Album, like many of the others known today, is inscribed and dated "Geo. Catlin./London 1852." The introductory text suggests that the drawings are "reduced from the original paintings and copied by my own hand." The two most similar albums—one at the Beinecke Rare Book and Manuscript Library of Yale University, comprising 216 pencil portraits in two bound volumes; and the other in The Newberry Library, Chicago, containing 217 pencil portraits which in recent years have been disbound[32]—are each similarly inscribed, contain portraits of individual sitters rather than groups, and include Indians who were not seen by Catlin until several years later. Catlin had traveled to South America, and along the coast of the Pacific Northwest, and into the northern Rocky Mountains between 1852 and 1855. In 1855 he took another jaunt to South

America.[33] It would seem logical then that the majority of the Souvenir Albums were not actually produced until after 1855.

In a letter introducing this Souvenir Album to the Duke of Portland, dated May 31, 1859, Catlin wrote, "This collection is entirely the work of my own hand and contains all the portraits which were seen in my collection at the Egyptian Hall, with the other tribes on the Pacific Coast, which I have visited at great expense and with great fatigue during the last three years, and which will be found to be of curious interest."

This clearly indicates that despite its 1852 inscription this album was actually completed after 1855. The Beinecke Library's Souvenir Album is also dated 1852, but a penciled inscription of "'57" is added. The Newberry Library's version, as mentioned above, includes Indians from the Northwest Coast, though it too is dated 1852.[34]

A close review of images from the three allied albums of drawings suggests that Catlin produced some of these drawings by tracing outlines or with the assistance of some lens device such as a *camera lucida*. In the Duke of Portland's album, the figures are generally situated in poses similar to those found in the original *Indian Gallery* collection. The portraits of *Mah-to-toh-pa* and *La-doo-ke-a* (figures 1 and 2) are exemplary when compared with the finished oil portraits in the *Indian Gallery* now owned by the Smithsonian Institution (figures 3 and 4). Aside from the fact that pencil drawings are not completed to full length, the angle of pose conforms well. In The Newberry Library album, these two portraits appear in reverse, as mirror images though nearly identical as copies[35] (figures 5 and 6). If the 1857 inscription is Catlin's, the Beinecke Library's versions may be the earliest and may have provided the images from which the Duke of Portland's were derived.[36] It is also very possible, given the nearly identical size and delineation of the images, that Catlin had in his possession by 1852 a set of templates from which these three albums (along with an album of 100 watercolors in the New York State Library in Albany) were traced. This could explain the seemingly erroneous dating of 1852.

Certain images in the Duke of Portland's album are divergent from the original portraits in the *Indian Gallery* in both pose and costume. The Blackfoot warrior *Iron Horn,* for example, appears in a half-length seated portrait adorned in a decorated quill shirt in the original gallery (figure 7). In the Duke of Portland's drawing, he is portrayed in a standing pose, cloaked with an elegant painted buffalo robe (figure 8). This presentation resembles more closely that of the same portrait in the Cartoon Collection group portrait of *Two Blackfoot Warriors and a Woman,* produced in oil after 1857 and now part of the Paul Mellon Collection in the National Gallery of Art (figure 9).

These Souvenir Albums appear to have met with varying success. Some, no doubt, were acquired with enthusiasm by English noblemen and institutions, thus accounting for the relatively large number of them. Others were turned back to the artist as inappropriate for consideration. For example, a two-volume set of drawings was offered to the British Museum by Catlin late in 1868 and returned with the explanation that the portfolio was "of great interest, but not *antique* enough for our institution."[37] The same portfolio was offered in 1869 to "the most aristocratic club in London," which was at the time, "collecting a vast library." When the drawings were returned, the rationale was quite the opposite of the British Museum's. The comment, as quoted in a letter from the artist to his brother Francis, was that the drawings "'are works of great historical interest, but *too old* — the Indian subject is getting too old.' How encouraging this," wrote Catlin, "and how droll — not old enough for one library and too old for another!"[38]

There were, of course, a long line of dukes of Portland. The one who bought Catlin's Souvenir Album which is published here was probably William John Cavendish Bentinch-Scott (1800–79), who was primarily known to history for his retiring habits of life. He no doubt did with the two albums exactly what Catlin feared might happen to his collection of oil paintings: the Duke returned them to his dusky mansion, effectively allowing the drawings to disappear from public view and appreciation, and displayed them only to a few select, curious visitors who might wander into his personal library. But for Catlin this sale provided income which permitted him to continue his work in pursuit of proper placement for his paintings.

It might be said that Catlin spent his last years working on and trying to market copies of his earlier life's *oeuvre.* This was not, certainly, what the artist would have hoped for, but it kept bread on the table and also was not exactly uncommon. Alfred Jacob Miller, for example, who had spent but one summer in the Far West in 1837, made a reasonable livelihood thereafter, reworking themes and compositions inspired by scenes encountered along the trek to and from the fur-trading rendezvous in the Wind River Mountains.

Catlin's original *Indian Gallery* lay dormant in a Philadelphia warehouse after being acquired by a locomotive manufacturer, Joseph Harrison, in 1852. Catlin had been forced to sell his collection that year because of severe indebtedness. Speculative investments, especially in Texas land, had gone sour, the *Indian Gallery* had not been acquired by Congress, and he had borrowed heavily on the promise that one or both of these schemes would succeed. Catlin was temporarily cast into debtors' prison, and once released he fled to Paris to escape his creditors. From France he made another urgent plea to Congress, which, as mentioned previously, failed. Harrison, who came through London that summer, paid off most of Catlin's debts, thereby assuming possession of the *Indian Gallery,* which would otherwise have been dispersed. He also shipped it back to Philadelphia and put the paintings in storage. Catlin was forced to start over.

As a means of invigoration, Catlin's subsequent trips to South America and the Far Northwest had provided some welcome new inspiration and images. These, along with the familiar subjects of earlier material, provided an ample supply of imagery for his final years. Although the several Souvenir Albums called for much of Catlin's time and energy, most effort was spent on two major projects — the Cartoon Collection, which numbered about 600 oils by the late 1860s, and what were called the "Outlines," a set of finished drawings completed after two and a half years of work in late 1868. These two sets he vigorously attempted to sell in America during the later years of his life. The Outlines were ultimately marketed for $750 (Catlin had hoped for $2,500) to the New-York Historical Society. This portfolio comprised, according to the artist's *Descriptive Catalogue of Catlin's Outlines of North American Indians,* "377 full-length portraits of North American Indians, and over 100 other designs, illustrating their manners and customs."[39] They may be considered the most ambitious of the Souvenir Albums. Catlin held them in such high regard that he made initial efforts to have Congress consider these in lieu of his *Indian Gallery.* Although he clearly preferred painting — as exemplified in his comment upon completion of the Outlines that "now I am G. Catlin again, look out for the paint"[40] — he professed great pride in his accomplishment as a draftsman. In his early thoughts about the Outlines, he perceived them as something which would substantially advance his artistic career. In fact he hoped to publish a portfolio, "to be executed in lines, in the best style of modern art."[41]

Despite the fact that the Outlines did not fetch the price he wished, Catlin was imbued with a sense of some gratification about them. They were the only major segment of his work which, during his lifetime, found its way into an American public collection. At least, he wrote his brother Francis, "they will be preserved in an Institution where they will be honourable memories of me when I am gone."[42] Later analysts of his work would even add to the importance of Catlin's drawings as art. Dr. Washington Matthews, in his defense of "The Catlin Collection of Indian Paintings," published in 1892, looked at drawing as the fundamental core of the artist's work. "Whatever unfavorable criticism may be made of Catlin as a colorist," he purported, "little disparagement can be made of his accuracy and spirit as a delineator."[43]

There has been much "disparagement" of Catlin over the years, some of it even about the accuracy of his work. The most telling negative remarks seem to have come during his lifetime from a man who had, early in the game, provided a glowing testimonial to the artist's credibility, Henry Schoolcraft. In the 1840 catalogue for Catlin's *Indian Gallery,* Schoolcraft, the Indian Agent for Wisconsin Territory, unequivocally endorsed the efforts of his colleague. "It gives me great pleasure," he extolled, "in being able to add my name to the list of those who have spontaneously expressed this approbation of Mr. Catlin's collection of Indian paintings." Schoolcraft claimed that Catlin's portraits "are drawn with great fidelity as to character and likeness."[44] However, in 1846, Schoolcraft attempted to persuade Catlin to lend selections from his *Indian Gallery* for purposes of illustration in his proposed monumental work on American Indian ethnology.[45] Catlin's refusal to cooperate won him the enduring disdain of Schoolcraft and subsequent negative critiques which left Catlin very much on the defensive. In support of his credence, Catlin commandeered some big guns and, in fact, received testimonials from the two biggest around — Baron Alexander von Humboldt, the greatest scientific mind of the century, and Prince Maximilian of Wied-Neuwied, Europe's most celebrated amateur adventurer.[46]

Perhaps Catlin's greatest defenders were the artists who followed in his footsteps, crediting him for their inspiration. The English painter of outdoor life, Arthur F. Tait, gathered his first impressions of the West from Catlin's images. He was persuaded by those to come to America and paint visions of frontier adventure which were ultimately translated into popular visual perceptions of the West by Currier & Ives. In equal measure, the *grande dame* of French painting, Rosa Bonheur, was intrigued by Catlin's images of Indians. Following the praise of Charles Baudelaire, who was attracted to Catlin's work in the 1846 Paris Salon, Bonheur took special notice of Catlin, eventually making dozens of copies of his work for her own use and pleasure. And, late in the century, Frederic Remington would claim that he started west with images of Catlin's work fresh in his mind.

If Remington viewed him as a mentor in 1881, almost a decade after Catlin died, what then was his role in American art? Back in 1833, when Catlin was showing his first legion efforts to the world, the *Western Monthly Magazine* of Cincinnati described his collection of paintings as "the most valuable addition to the history of our continent as well as to the arts of our country."[47] He was part of the Romantic movement as it melded with the Realist tradition in the early nineteenth century. His romance was professed in the vision of a disappearing race; his realism was manifest in his efforts to document those people before their demise. His portraits were true enough to be recognized by and bring tears to the eyes of the children and the grandchildren of the departed heroes represented.[48] For modern observers, "a Catlin Crow is a Crow, a Catlin Mandan is a Mandan, and the differentiation is important."[49]

Beyond Catlin's place as an artist and writer and provoker of a national conscience, he must be summarily recognized as one of America's greatest visionaries. Working originally under the pressure of time and the inconvenience of circumstance, he produced the grandest scheme for cultural preservation and individual artistic expression ever conceived in this nation. And the results speak well for the effort. His quest was sufficient for one lifetime. As he said it, "the history and customs of such a people, preserved by pictorial illustrations, are themes worthy of the lifetime of one man, and nothing, short of the loss of my life, shall prevent me from visiting their country and of becoming their historian."[50] Our life is the richer for it.

PETER H. HASSRICK
Director of the Buffalo Bill Historical Center
Cody, Wyoming

Figure 1: *Mandan, Mah-to-toh-pa (the Four Bears)...,* pencil on paper, c. 1857,
14″ × 10½″, Duke of Portland Album (No. 108).

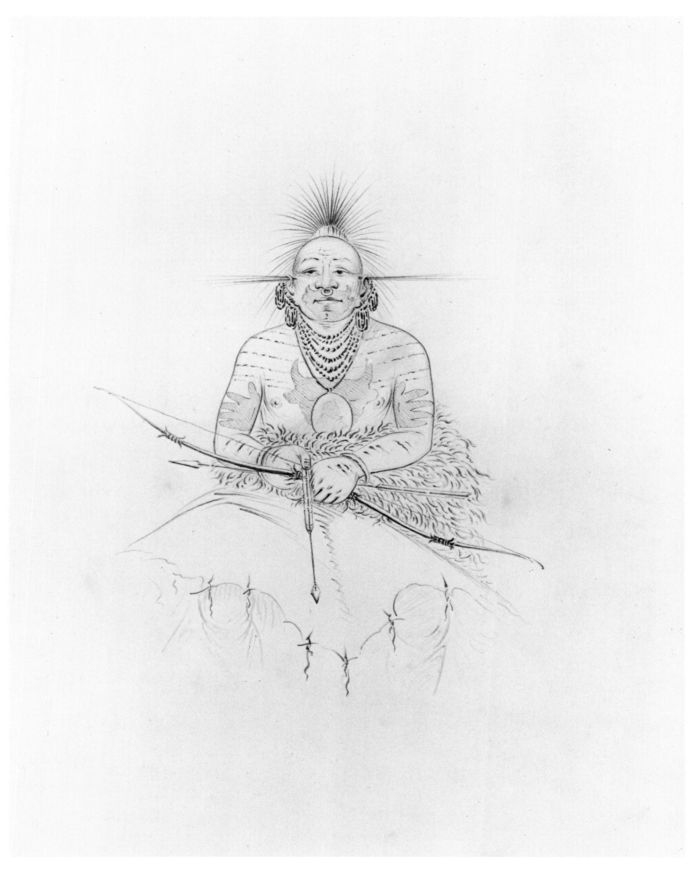

Figure 2: *Pawnee, La-doo-ke-a (the Buffalo Bull)...*, pencil on paper, c. 1857, 14″ × 10½″, Duke of Portland Album (No. 1).

Figure 3: *Four Bears, Second Chief in Full Dress,* oil on canvas, 1832, 29″ × 24″, National Museum of American Art, Smithsonian Institution, Washington, D.C. Gift of Mrs. Joseph Harrison, Jr.

Figure 4: *Buffalo Bull, a Grand Pawnee Warrior,* oil on canvas, 1832, 29″ × 24″, National Museum of American Art, Smithsonian Institution, Washington, D.C. Gift of Mrs. Joseph Harrison, Jr.

Figure 5: *Mandan, Mah-to-toh-pa (the Four Bears)...,* pencil on paper, c. 1855, 9⅛″ × 5⅞″. Courtesy of the Edward E. Ayer Collection, The Newberry Library Album, Chicago (No. 47).

Figure 6: *Pawnee, La-du-kee-a (the Buffalo Bull)...,* pencil on paper, c. 1855, 9⅛″ × 5⅞″. Courtesy of the Edward E. Ayer Collection, The Newberry Library Album, Chicago (No. 106).

Figure 7: *Iron Horn, a Warrior (Blackfoot),* oil on canvas, 1832, 29″ × 24″, National Museum of American Art, Smithsonian Institution, Washington, D.C. Gift of Mrs. Joseph Harrison, Jr.

Figure 8: *Blackfoot, Mix-ke-mote-skin-na (the Iron Horn)...,* pencil on paper, c. 1857, 9⅛″ × 5⅞″, Duke of Portland Album (No. 127).

Figure 9: *Two Blackfoot Warriors and a Woman,* oil on cardboard, 1857/69, 17½″ × 23½″, Paul Mellon Collection, National Gallery of Art, Washington, D.C.

FOOTNOTES

1. See Ron Tyler, ed., *Alfred Jacob Miller: Artist on the Oregon Trail* (Fort Worth: Amon Carter Museum, 1982), p. 4; and J.N.B. Hewitt, ed., *Journal of Rudolph Friederich Kurz* (Washington, D.C.: Smithsonian Institution, 1937), p. 130.

2. Henry T. Tuckerman, *Book of the Artists* (New York: James F. Carr Publisher, 1967), pp. 426–27.

3. William Dunlap, *A History of the Rise and Progress of the Arts of Design in the United States,* Vol. II, Part 2 (New York: Dover Publications, 1969 reprint), p. 378.

4. George Catlin, *Letters and Notes on the Manners, Customs, and Condition of the North American Indians,* Vol. I (London: David Bogue, 1844), p. 2.

5. Ibid., p. 3.

6. Ibid., p. 263.

7. Ibid., Vol. II, p. 196.

8. Ibid.

9. Numerous scholars have discussed Catlin's itinerary of western travel and the dates when Catlin printed the various views and portraits. Probably the most reliable and up-to-date version appears in William H. Truettner, *The Natural Man Observed: A Study of Catlin's Indian Gallery* (Washington, D.C.: Smithsonian Institution, 1979).

10. Catlin, *Letters and Notes,* Vol. I, p. 15.

11. Ibid.

12. Quoted in "Catlin, the Painter of Indians," *The Arkansas Gazette,* September 23, 1834.

13. Harold McCracken, *George Catlin and the Old Frontier* (New York: Bonanza Books, 1959), p. 188.

14. Quoted in McCracken, *George Catlin,* p. 189.

15. George Catlin, *Catlin's Notes of Eight Years' Travels and Residence in Europe...,* Vol. I (published by author as his *Indian Collection No. 6,* Waterloo Place, London, 1848), p. v.

16. Ibid., pp. 1–2.

17. London *Times,* February 3, 1840.

18. *Catlin's Notes of Eight Years' Travels,* Vol. I, p. 90.

19. Ibid.

20. Quoted in Thomas Donaldson, "The George Catlin Indian Gallery in the U.S. National Museum," *Smithsonian Report,* Part II (1885), p. 781.

21. John C. Ewers, *George Catlin, Painter of Indians and the West* (Washington, D.C.: Smithsonian Institution, 1956), p. 491.

22. R.R. Gurley, *Memorial of R.R. Gurley Praying the Purchase of Catlin's Collection of Paintings and Curiosities...* (Washington, D.C.: U.S. Government Printing Office, 1848), pp. 1–2.

23. Tyler, *Alfred Jacob Miller,* p. 4.

24. Hewitt, *Journal,* p. 130.

25. "Panoramas in London," *Bulletin of the American Art-Union,* June 1850.

26. Gurley, *Memorial,* p. 2.

27. *Catlin's Notes of Eight Years' Travels,* p. 35.

28. See Truettner, *The Natural Man,* p. 53.

29. Marjorie Catlin Roehm, *The Letters of George Catlin and His Family* (Berkeley, Calif.: University of California Press, 1966), p. 310.

30. Ibid., p. 451.

31. Truettner, *The Natural Man,* pp. 133–34.

32. Each of these two portfolios carries the identical title as the Duke of Portland's — *SOUVENIR OF THE NORTH AMERICAN INDIANS as they were, in the middle of the 19th century, a numerous and noble race of HUMAN BEINGS fast passing to extinction and leaving no monuments of their own behind them.*

33. Marvin C. Ross, *George Catlin: Episodes from Life Among the Indians and Last Rambles* (Norman, Okla.: University of Oklahoma Press, 1959), p. xx.

34. Other Souvenir Albums which fit this description but contain primarily multiple portraits in pencil are listed below:

The New York Public Library has a portfolio with the title *Souvenir of the North American Indians,* which is signed by Catlin and inscribed "London, 1850." There are 167 pencil drawings in three folios. Several of the portraits depict tribes of America's West Coast not visited by Catlin until well after 1850.

The Montana Historical Society has an album entitled *Souvenir of the North American Indians as they were, in the middle of the 19th century.* It is signed and inscribed "Geo. Catlin, London, 1852." Many of the 120 pencil portraits depict Indians which Catlin did not see until after his trip to America's West Coast, which would suggest that Catlin's date is erroneous and that the portfolio would have been completed some time after 1855.

The Museum of Mankind, the Ethnography Department of the British Museum, has a similar album dated 1861. Two folio volumes contain 159 pencil drawings.

A fourth album, comprising 100 drawings and dated 1852, is part of the New York State Library collections in Albany. The plates contained in that album closely resemble those in the Duke of Portland and the Beinecke Rare Book and Manuscript Library albums. The portraits are half-length watercolors over pencil drawings for the most part. In regard to medium and in the fact that the underlying drawing is somewhat unresolved by comparison, the Albany album is quite unique. In fact, Catlin made a special note at the end of his introductory remarks to that album alluding to its singularity — "there is no duplicate of this album in existence."

35. Catlin discussed, on at least one occasion, the use of photographic lenses in the reduction of his works during later years. See Roehm, *Letters,* p. 450.

36. Truettner, *The Natural Man,* p. 134, points out that tracing was the common means of reproducing the essential images of these albums.

37. Roehm, *Letters,* p. 379. The Museum of Mankind, the ethnography Department of the British Museum, now owns one of the Souvenir Albums, composed of 159 pencil drawings in two folio volumes and dated 1861. It may be the same as the one they turned down.

38. Ibid.

39. Richard J. Koke, *American Landscape and Genre Paintings in the New-York Historical Society,* Vol. I (New York: New-York Historical Society, 1982), p. 142.

40. Roehm, *Letters,* p. 369.

41. Ibid., p. 348.

42. Koke, *American Landscape,* p. 152.

43. Washington Matthews, "The Catlin Collection of Indian Paintings," *Report of the National Museum for 1890* (Washington, D.C.: U.S. Government Printing Office, 1892), pp. 593–610.

44. Catlin, *Descriptive Catalogue of Catlin's Indian Gallery,* p. 5.

45. Henry Rowe Schoolcraft, *Historical and Statistical Information Regarding the History, Conditions, and Prospects of the Indian Tribes of the United States,* 6 vols. (Philadelphia: Lippincott, Grambo, 1851–57).

46. Roehm, *Letters,* p. 345.

47. Quoted in Byron B. Jones, "George Catlin: His Impossible Dream," *Southwest Art,* May 1982, p. 123.

48. Matthews, "The Catlin Collection," p. 602.

49. Bernard DeVoto, *Across the Wide Missouri* (Boston: The Houghton Mifflin Company, 1947), p. 395.

50. Catlin, *Letters and Notes,* Vol. I, p. 2.

THE
DRAWINGS

His Grace

The Duke of Portland,

London.

His Grace The Duke of Portland,

My Lord,

I have taken the liberty of Sending
for your inspection, what no other person on
earth can Send you ; two volumes of por-
-traits of N. Am. Indians, illustrating all
the tribes in N.Amᵃ both in British and
united States Territories.

This collection is entirely the work
of my own hand, and contains all
the portraits which were seen in my collection
at the Egyptian Hall, with the other
tribes on the Pacific coast, which I have
visited at great expense, and with great
fatigue, during the last 3 years, and which
will be found to be of curious interest.

These drawings were reduced from my original
paintings with the greatest care, with the
view of publishing in that form, but
which plan I have abandoned. And if

Your Lordship should feel disposed to possess and perpetuate these Records of these abused and fast vanishing Races, whose looks & customs I have devoted the best part of my life, and all my means, in rescuing from oblivion. I know of no one into whose hands I should feel more satisfied to place them, and for the moderate price of £75.

I could not afford to repeat such labour for a less price than £ 175.

If the Drawings should not be retained, I hope they will afford sufficient amusement to excuse the liberty I have taken, And beg that one of Your Lordships Servants may be instructed to send them to me by Pickford, to care of Pickford & Co. which is also my address. Dover

Your Lordships Obedient Servant
Geo. Catlin.
Dover 31st May/59.

P.S. These Drawings are quite imperishable the Crayons being so fixed as not to soil, even by rubbing the hand over them,

G.C.

SOUVENIR

OF THE

NORTH AMERICAN INDIANS,

as they were in the middle of the 19th century ;

a numerous and noble race of

HUMAN BEINGS,

fast passing to extinction,

and leaving no monuments of their own behind them.

Having become fully convinced of the certain extinction of the N. Am: native Races, I resolved, at an early period of my life, to make and preserve for future ages, as far as my individual labours and personal means would enable me to do, a pictorial history of these interesting people; and with this view have, with great fatigue and privation, (and with the most complete success) visited 50. tribes, mostly speaking different languages. From among these tribes I have brought home a very extensive collection of portraits, and other paintings, illustrating their modes of living and customs; the portraits of which collection are contained in these two volumes, reduced from the original paintings, & copied by my own hands.   Geo. Catlin.

London. 1852.

Remark.

The costumes, weapons, &c in the following series of portraits, however strange or incredible they may seem, are strict representations, even to the most minute or trivial ornament, as worn by the individuals who sat or stood for the portraits.

The 215. portraits contained in these two vols. embrace all the tribes residing in British and U. States Territories, both East and West of the Rocky Mountains, all of which I have visited, and painted my portraits from the life, by their own firesides.

In endeavouring to rescue from oblivion the looks and customs of these vanishing Races, I have de-voted the best part of my life, and all my earthly means, and in justice to these poor people, let it be as imperishable as these designs, that amongst two millions, where I have travelled unprotected, they every where treated me with honour and with kindness.

Geo. Catlin.

Tribes Represented.

50

Pawnee — Konza — Sioux — Crow —
Ojibbeway — Winnebago — Kioway —
Mandan — Assinneboin — Blackfoot
Shienne — Riccarree — Minatarree
Puncah — Ottoe Shawano — Saukie —
Camanchee — Wico — Pawnee Pict. —
Ioway — Seneca — Oneida — Delaware —
Tuskarora — Micmac — Iroquois — Nayas —
Flathead — Nez percé — Arapaho — Snake —
Navaho — Apachee — Peoria — Weeah —
Kaskaskia — Kickapoo — Potowatomie
Mohigan — Choctaw — Creek — Osage —
Omaha — Missouri — Knisteneux —
Menomonie — Seminolee — Cherokee —
Piankeshaw.

Pawnee

I a-doo-ke-a (the Buffalo Bull) one of the most celebrated Warriors of the Pawnee tribe, in his war dress & war paints, and wrapped in his Buffalo Robe, drawing his Bow. The Buffalo Bull being his totem, he has its head painted on his breast and on his face, when he goes to war.

The Pawnee tribe contains about 10.000, & its position is on the River Platte, between the Mississippi and the base of the Rocky Mountains. N. lat. 43. & 44°.

Pawnee

Le-shaw-loo-lah-le-hoo. (the Big Elk) a secondary chief, wearing a beautifully ornamented Robe, and Smo--king a long and handsome pipe. his head dress made of War Eagles plumes.

As the War Eagle of that country Con--quers all other varieties of the Eagle Spe--cies the Indians set a high value on the tail feathers of that valiant bird, to adorn the heads of the brave, none others are allowed to wear them.

3

Pawnee

La-nee-tees-(——————) a Pawnee Woman, wife of the chief, on the foregoing page, with her infant (pap--poose) in its beautifully ornamented cradle.

All the tribes in N. Am. carry their infants on their backs in cradles; the backs of which are straight boards, to which the infants backs are lashed, causing straight and healthy figures And preventing deformities of the spine, which are never seen amongst the N. Am. Indians.

4

Pawnee

Shon-ka-ki-hee-ga (the Horse Chief) called also, "We-tar-ra-sha-ro" head Chief of the Pawnees, in a magnificent dress, with his tomahawk in his hand.

This dignified chief was the host and protector of the Hon. C. A. Murray (afterwards Master of Her Majesties Household) while he was on a visit to the Pawnees, in 1833. See "Murray's Tour to the Pawnees." 2 vols. oct°—"

Pawnee

Ah-sha-la-coots-a (the Mole in the forehead) a distin-guished Warrior, wearing a handsome Robe, and holding his Bow and arrows in his hand.

The Pawnee tribe shave the head, leaving only a small patch of hair on the crown, to which they attach a beautiful red Crest, made of the hair of the deer's tail dyed red, and horse hair.

6

Pawnee

L'har-ree-tar-rushe (the ill natured Man) a celebra-
-ted Warrior, in full War Costume, with his pipe toma-
-hawk in his hands, and a horse-whip attached to
his wrist.

Every Warrior has some peculiar mode
of painting his face and his limbs when he
goes to war, & which is called his "Warpaint". And when these portraits were
painted, it being considered an honour
conferred on them, none but the
brave were allowed by the chiefs,
to have their portraits made, and they
then generally arrayed themselves in
their War Costume, & war paint.

7

Pawnee

Loo-ra-wee-re-coo (the bird that goes to War) a famous Warrior, in War costume and War paint, with his tomahawk in his hand, and wearing an ornamented and honourable Robe, with his battles painted out.

As the Indians neither read nor write, there are no public Records kept, leaving it necessary therefore for each individual to Record his battles in the best way that he can, which is done by pictorial representations on their Robes, & also by taking and preserving the scalps of their victims slain in battle.

8

Omaha

Nom-ba-mon-ye (the double Walker) a celebrated warrior of the Omaha tribe, beautifully dressed, and equipped for War. his Bow & arrows in his hand, and a panthers Skin quiver Slung on his back. and his neck lace made of the enormous paw of a grizly Bear.

A Small tribe, West side of the Mississippi. N. lat. 45°

Omaha

Om-pa-ton-ga - (the Big Elk) a noted Warrior, dressed, equipped & ready for War. wrapped in his Robe, with his bow and arrows clenched under it, ready at a moments notice.

Omaha.

Man-sha-qui-ta- (the little Soldier) a beautiful
Warrior, elegantly equipped and painted, with his shield
and quiver slung, and his Bow & arrows & War club
in his hands, And his beautiful kilt, made of the
War Eagles plumes.

Omaha

Ki-ho-ga-wa-shu-shee. (the very Brave chief) head chief of the tribe, with a magnificent costume and equipments. his shield And panther-skin quiver slung on his back — a splendid Robe crosses his left shoulder, And he holds in his left hand a long and beautiful pipe, His necklace is made of the Grisly Bears Claws; and his head dress of the War Eagles plumes, Surmounted by a pair of horns, denoting his power, as head War Chief of the tribe.

(like an ancient Jewish custom)

12

Omaha

O-nah-mee- (———) an Omaha woman, wife of the chief, on the foregoing page. In a very beautiful dress, with her Eagle tail fan in her hand.

13

Konza

Sho–me–cos–see (the Wolf) head chief of the Konza tribe, in a beautiful costume, wearing a Robe, with a Buffalo hunt represented on it, and smoking a long and handsome pipe, the stem beautifully embroi- dered with porcupine quills, and the bowl made of the red pipe stone.

A tribe of 6. or 7,000. S.W. of the Missouri, in lat. 42°. n. This tribe has recently Surrendered an immense tract of country, rapidly settled and formed into a new state.

14

Konza

Wa-hon-ga-shee (not a fool) a celebrated Warrior,
wrapped in his Robe, with his tomahawk on his arm.

Konza

Chesh–oo–hong–ha (the man of good sense) a very elegant young man, curiously dressed, ornamented & equipped for war.

This tribe, like the Pawnees, already mentioned, shave the head, and ornament it with the Red Crest, with a helmet shape.

Konza

Meach-o-shin-gaw. (the Little White Bear) Said to be the most desperate and successful warrior in the tribe: terrible and cruel with his enimies, but kind and honourable to his friends. fully equipped and armed for battle. his shield on his arm, his Bow in his hands, and Scalping knife worn under his belt.

17

Konza

(———————) a Konza woman, wife of the chief (nº 13.) wearing a great profusion of beads & Wampum.

18

Sioux

Wa-e-ton. (————) chief of the Susseton Band of Sioux. A very distinguished man, in a magnificent costume; his head dress of War Eagles quills, descending to the ground, and his necklace made of the claws of the Grizzly Bear

The Sioux is one of the most powerful tribes in N. Am. about 25,000. occupying a vast tract of country on the Upper Mississippi & Missouri Rivers, and hunting quite to the base of the Rocky Mountains.

19

Sioux

(————————) a Warrior of the Sisseton Band,
with his Shield and quiver slung, & his lance in his
hand.

Sioux

Nee_ne (————————) a Sioux girl, unmarried, daughter of the Chief Waneton, (no 18) in a very pretty dress. the Tunique made of two mountain Sheep skins, and the Robe from the skin of a young Buffalo.

Sioux

Mah-to-chee-ga (the Little Bear) a very famous Warrior, wrapped in a beautiful Robe, his Shield on his back, and his pipe tom a hawk in his hand.

Sioux

Shonka — (the Dog) chief of a Band, said
to be very famous as a Warrior, curiously draped,
and holding a Calumet (pipe of peace) in his
hand.

All Indians Smoke, and each one
manufactures his own pipe, after his
own peculiar taste or fancy. The Calumet
is a sacred pipe, ornamented with
Eagles quills — always in the Chiefs
possession, and only used at Treaties,
which are solemnized by Smoking through
the "Sacred Stem"

23

Sioux

Tah-teck-a-da hair (the Sleep wind) a young
Warrior, said to be celebrated . his Bow and quiver
Slung on his back .

24

Sioux.

wa-nah-de-tunk-a (the Black Dog) Chief of
a Band, on the St. Peters River, with a hand-
-some pipe in his hand. This man has been
much admired by white people, as well as by
his own tribe, for his dignity of character &
eloquence in council.

Sioux

(———————) the Red Wing) chief of a band of Sioux, on the Mississippi River, below the Falls of St Anthony. A man celebrated for his terrible battles with the Ojibbeways.

Sioux

Toh-to-wa-con-da-pee (the Blue Medicine)
a famous Medicine Man (Doctor) living at St Peters.
Falls of St. Anthony, with his Medicine (mystery)
drum and rattle in his hands — his medicine bag,
skin of a Badger, attached to his belt, and
his Eagle tail fan fastened to his wrist.

Sioux

(———————) a Sioux woman, wife of the chief (no. 24) suckling her child four years old, not an unusual occurrence among the N. Am⯑ Indians.

This custom, with that of marrying at a premature age (from 12. to 14 years) is probably the cause of the comparatively small number of children borne by the Indian women, they seldom bearing more than 3 or 4.

28

Sioux

Ee-ah-sa-pa (the Black Rock) head War chief of the Sioux tribe, in a magnificent dress — his head dress of Ermine and Eagles quills, descending to the ground, and surmounted by horns, denoting his power, as head War chief of his Tribe.

This curious custom I have found to exist in every tribe, and but one man in the tribe Can wear them. And as before remarked, it Seems to be decidedly like an ancient Jewish Custom.

29

Sioux

Wi-loo-ta-hee-tchah-ta-ma-nee. (the red thing that touches the ground in marching) An unmarried girl, daughter of the War chief, on the foregoing page, in a beautiful dress, wearing a Robe made of a young Buffalo's skin.

30

Sioux

S'tcha-nee. (——————) a Sioux woman, wife of the War chief, (no. 28) with her infant (pappoose) in its beautiful cradle, carried on her back.

All the N. Am. tribes carry their infants on their backs, lashed to a straight board. This apparently cruel mode is ingenious, inasmuch as it enables the woman to labour with her hands, whilst her infant is rocked, and sleeps on her back. And no doubt promotes straightness and healthiness of the spine, diseases and deformi- ties of which are not met with amongst the N. Am. Indians.

31

Sioux

Ha-wan-je-tah - (the One Horn) head chief of the Sioux tribe, seated on the ground, in a splendid dress, richly garnished with porcupine quill embroidery, and profusely fringed with scalp locks, and smoking a long and handsome pipe.

The Sioux tribe is divided into 40. Bands; each band having a chief at its head, all of whom, when seated in Council with this head chief, form the Government of the nation.

Sioux

(——————————) A Sioux woman, wife of the Chief, on the foregoing page, with her infant in its cradle, her dress curiously ornamented with beads and brass buttons.

Sioux

Tchon-dee - (Tobacco) Second chief of the Sioux tribe, and very distinguished for his feats of bravery, Seated on the ground, with his shield and lance before him - his shirt and leggins beautifully embroidered with porcupine quills. and fringed with scalp locks.

The porcupine (hedge hog) of that country produces a great quantity of short, white quills, which the In- -dians dye of various brilliant colours, and highly value to ornament their dresses.

"Scalp locks"— As these people neither read nor write, they have no public Records of their battles & victories; and each Warrior is expected to preserve the Record for himself, which he does by taking a small patch of the skin from the crown of the head of his victim, which he preserves, and calls a "scalp"— the remainder of his victims hair fringes his shirt and leggins, with "scalp locks"

34

Sioux

Toh-ki-e-to- (the Stone with horns) the great Medi-
-cine-Man and counsellor of the Chief, seated on the
ground, with a beautiful pipe in his hand, and tobacco
pouch before him — his breast and arms curiously tat-
-tooed, a custom but seldom practiced amongst the N.
Am. Indians.

The numerous marks and devices seen on the
bodies and limbs & faces, of most of these portraits
are caused by vermillion and other bright colours,
mixed with Bear's grease, and plastered on
in the morning, to be removed at night.

35

Osage

T'chong—tas—sab—bee. (the Black Dog) the War—chief of the Osages; a man of six feet and a half in stature, and corpulent at the same time, with a beautiful pipe in one hand, and his tomahawk, with a scalp attached, in the other.

This tribe has been terrible in War with its enemies, but always friendly to civilized people. They are now reduced to 3. or 4.000. occupying a large range of Country, North of the Arkansas, lat. N. 33. & 34°

36

Osage

Tal—lee - (———————) One of the most famous of the Osage Warriors, always at the side of the War Chief, with whom he was the favourite; fully dressed and equipped for War.

37.

Osage.

Ko-ha-tunka (the Big Crow) a young Warrior,
in War costume, with shield and quiver slung, and
tomahawk in his hand.

This tribe, like the Pawnees & Konzas, shave the
head, and ornament it with the red crest.

Osage

Cler-mont. (——————) head chief of the Osage tribe; seated, and holding his War cleeb on his arm.

No one can justly estimate the gentlemanly elegance of this graceful chief, without entering his hospitable wigwam, and taking him by the hand, as the Author has done.

Osage

Mun‗ne‗pus‗kee (he who is not afraid) a very fine young Warrior, in War Costume, a great favourite of the chief.

40

Osage

Nah-com-e-shee (Man of the Bed) a distinguished Young Warrior, in War costume — resting on his lance .

Osage

wah–chee–te (—————) An Osage woman, wife of Cler–mont, the head chief, (no. 38) with her child in her arms.

Ojibbeway

Ka-bes-kunk (he who travels everywhere) a handsome young Warrior, in War dress and warpaint, holding his lance in his hands.

The Ojibbeway is one of the most numerous and powerful tribes in N. Am. occupying a vast tract of country, both in British and U. States Territories, on the head waters of the Mississippi and shores of Lake Superior.

Ojibbeway

O-ta-wa (the Ottoway) a very famous young Warrior, holding his War club and medicine bag in one hand; and his pipe and tobacco pouch in the other.

44

Ojibbeway

Ju-a-kis-gaw (— — — —) an Ojibbeway woman
wife of the Warrior (no 42) with her infant (pappoose) in
its cradle

Ojibbeway

Gitch—ee—gaw—ga—osh. (the point that remains forever)
an aged chief, of great celebrity, with his pipe in
his hand.

Ojibbeway

On-daig- (the Crow) a young man, seated, with his fan in his hand, made of an Eagle's tail, curiously dressed and ornamented, and supposed to partake more of the Beau than of the Warrior.

Ojibbeway

I-an-be-wa-dick. (the male Caribou) a beautiful
and gallant little Warrior, Seated on the ground, with
his Bow & arrows in his hand.

Ojibbeway

Sha-co-pay (the Six -) (the killer of Six) head Chief of the Tribe, in a splendid dress, ornamented with a profusion of Scalp locks.

The Ojibbeway tribe, like the Sioux, has a great number of Bands — each Band has its Chief, all of whom are subordinate to this Chief.

Ojibbeway

(——————————) An Ojibbeway woman, wife of
the Chief, on the foregoing page.

Camanchee

His—oo—san—chees. (——————) one of the most
famous Warriors of the Camanchee tribe, in full
War Costume and War paint.

The Camanchees, of 10.000. are amongst the
most Warlike and powerful tribes in N. Am,
residing on the head waters of the Red River
and Arkansas. lat. n. 33.34°.

Camanchee.

Ta-wa-que-nah. (the mountain of Rocks) one of the principal chiefs of the Camanchees; a man extremely corpulent, and with a sparce beard on his chin, both of which are exceedingly rare amongst the N. Am. tribes.

Camanchee

(———————) A Camanchee woman, wife of the Chief, on the fore going page, with her fan in her hand.

Camanchee

Ee-sha-ko-nee (the Bow & Quiver) head chief of the Camanchee tribe, seated on the ground, and smoking a handsome pipe, with his shield and lance before him.

Camanchee

Ha-nee (the Beaver) one of the chiefs of the Camanchees, celebrated for his successful battles with the Osages, seated on the ground, with his bow and pipe in his hands.

Camanchee

Is–sa–wah–tam–a (the wolf tied with hair) a desperate Warrior, seated on the ground, with his bow and tomahawk in his hand .

Camanchee

(————— -)

(————— -) Two Camanchee children,
daughters of the chief (no 51)

57.

Wico

Ush-ee-kitz (he who fights with a feather) head chief of the tribe — a humane and excellent man.

A small tribe, on the extreme sources of the Red River, in Texas. lat. N. 32° —

Wico

(————————) a Wico woman, wife and child of the chief on the foregoing page.

Wico

Kots-a-to-ah (——————) a distinguished Warrior of the tribe, with his lance in his hand.

Flathead

Hoogst-ah-a (———— ————) Second chief of the tribe, almost hidden in the curious folds of his blanket, but still, perfectly illustrating the unaccountable custom of flattening the head, by an artificial process, practiced in that tribe

A numerous, but not warlike, tribe, inhabiting the lower parts of the Columbia River, on the Pacific Coast.

Flathead

Michst. (——————) a Flathead Woman, wife of the chief, on the foregoing page, basketing Salmon, at the Dalles, on the Columbia River. — Carrying her infant in its cradle, on her back, while it is undergoing the process of flattening the head.

Flathead

Ya-tax-ta-coo (———————) a young Warrior, said to be distinguished, with the head flattened, though Custom of flattening the head is confined, almost entirely, to the women.

Flathead

Yun-ne-yow. (the green vine that creeps) a Boy of 14. years, with his salmon Bow, — his head flattened. Salmon are killed in vast quantities, while passing up the Rapids, in the Dalles, by the Indians, who stand perched upon the rocks above, and shoot there with their harpoon arrows.

Flathead

(———————————) A Flathead woman, seated on the ground, with her infant in its crib, or cradle, undergoing the process of flattening the head.

The flattening process commences immediately after the child is born, and lasts from two to three months, when it is taken out and carried on the back, or under the arm. This ridiculous and disgust -ing custom seems to have no other object then that of beautifying their looks, nor does it appear, in any way to impair their intellects or general health.

65

Snake

Yau-nau-shau-pix (——————) one of the
chiefs of the tribe, distinguished by his desperate
battles with the Crow Indians. He wears the Robe
of a distinguished Crow Chief whom he slew in
single combat — his head dress a very beautiful one,
made of Ermine and War Eagle quills.

A small, but warlike tribe, on the
head Waters of the Columbia River.
lat. N. 40°

Snake

Naw-en-saw-pec (he who runs up hill) a Warrior. Said to be celebrated, wrapped in his Buffalo Robe, with his quiver slung on his back.

Snake.

On-da-wout. (the smooth bark) a very distin-
-guished Warrior, wearing a very beautiful Robe,
with his quiver slung on his back.

Shyenne

Nee-hee-o-woo-tis. (the wolf on the hill) chief of the tribe, in a beautiful costume, holding a long and very beautiful pipe in his hand.

A tribe of 5. or 6.000. residing at the East base of the Rocky Mountains, between the Platte and Yellow Stone Rivers, lat. N. 46° -

Shyenne

(——————) A Shyenne woman, wife of the chief, on the foregoing page, in a very pretty dress, made of mountain sheeps skins.

Shyenne

Hee-won-e-tax. (——————) the great orator, and wise man of the tribe, Doctor, and Counsellor to the Chief.

Kiowa

Teeh-toot-sa. (———) head chief of his tribe, and said to be a very distinguished man.

A small tribe, of 2.000. residing at the E. base of the Rocky Mountains, head waters of the Red River, of Texas

Kiowa

Bon-son-jee. (the new fire) a famous Warrior, and favourite of the chief, in War dress and War paint, with his war club in his hand.

Kiowa

(——————)

(——————) a Kioway young woman and Boy,
Brother and Sister – children of the Chief.

Delaware

Bod-a-sin (————) Chief of the Tribe, & a very distinguished man.

But a remnant, of this once numerous & warlike tribe now exist — they are chiefly civilized, and have been removed to a country far West of the Mississippi.

Delaware

Non-on-da-gon. (——————————) Second chief
of the delawares, a dignified and gentlemanly
man.

Delaware.

(—————————) a Delaware woman, wife of the Chief, (N⁰ 74)

Creek

Stu-cha-co-me-co (the Great King) called "Ben Perryman", one of the chiefs of the tribe, with his Rifle in his hand.

A tribe of 15.000. partly civilized, & recently removed from the State of Georgia, to the Arkansas. 700. miles W. of the Mississippi.

Creek

Hol-te-mal-te-tez-te-neek-e (—————————) Called "Sam Perryman", Brother of the Chief on the foregoing page. A gentlemanly and excellent man, known to be a stern advocate for temperance, in his tribe.

Tuskarora

Cusick — (———————) Son of the chief — civilized and Christianized. This man was a Baptist prea- -cher in his tribe, when the portrait was painted.

Mic Mac

Ho-neet-gosh (——————) a Mic mac hunter and Warrior, with his Rifle in his hand.

in Eastern Canada, the remnant of a numerous & warlike tribe, civilized and mostly agricultural.

Mohigan

Ee-tow-o-kaum (both sides of the River)
chief of the tribe, — civilized and Christianized,
with his psalm book in one hand, and his cane
in the other.

Shawano

Lay-law-shee-kaw. (he who goes up the River)
An aged man, and chief of the tribe ; the rims
of his ears curiously separated and elongated.

This tribe, once numerous and warlike,
occupied a great proportion of the State of
Pennsylvania ; but have been fought
and removed, until they are but a
small remnant, living several
hundred miles W. of the Mississippi.

Shawano

Kay-tee-qua (the female Eagle) a Shawano girl, unmarried, daughter of the chief, on the foregoing page .

Shawano

Pah-te-coo-saw. (the Straight man) a young man of the tribe, not known to be distinguished.

Shawano.

'Ten-squa-ta-way (the open door) this man, blind in his right eye, was Brother to the famous Tecumseh, and is represented with his "sacred string of beans" in one hand, and his "miraculous fire" in the other, by the mysterious influence of which he succeeded in raising 30.000. Warriors for Tecumseh, amongst the neighbouring hostile tribes, to act in concert against the approaching civilized frontier.

Navaho

Tchongs-tee (the Singer) a young Warrior, Said to have achieved a great deal by his battles with the Snake Indians.

A small tribe, inhabiting the Rocky Mountains, on the extreme Sources of the Colorado of the West.

Navaho

Na-qua-sab-bee. (not afraid of any one) a young
Warrior, in War Costume and equipments.

Navaho

(—————) a Navaho woman, mother of the two young men in the two foregoing pages.

Oneida

(——————————) Bread) Chief of the tribe, a remarkeably fine young man, And an advocate for Temperance. Civilized.

The remnant of a powerful tribe, in the Western part of the State of New York.

Oneida

(———————) An Oneida young woman, Sister of the young chief, on the foregoing page.

Pun_cah

Shoo_de_gha_cha. (Smoke) chief of the tribe, a remarkeably dignified and philanthropic man, wrapped in his Buffalo Robe, and holding his lance in his hand.

A small tribe, of 2.000. on the W_ bank of the Missouri. Lat. N. 43° _

Puncah

Hongs-kay-dee. (the great chief) oldest Son of the chief, & heir apparent.

The Author was present when this young Prince of 18. years was married to four wives at the Same moment, in presence of the whole tribe. The four girls were all daughters of Subordinate chiefs, & apparently all between the ages of 12. and 14 years.

Puncah

Mong-shong-shaw. (the bending Willow) in a beautiful dress — one of the four wives of the gallant Young Prince, painted the day after she was married.

Puncah.

Hee-lah-dee- (the pure fountain) the mother of Hongs-Kay-dee, the gallant young Prince, and wife of the Chief (no. 91.) Her heart and arms curiously tattooed, a custom but seldom practiced by the N. Am. tribes.

Minatarree

Eehk-tohk-pa-shee-pee-shaw. (the Black Mocasin) head chief of the tribe, said to have been 105. years old when the portrait was painted. Seated, and smoking a handsome pipe, with his Robe wrapped around him.

A small tribe, of 2.000. on the W. bank of the Missouri. 2.000. miles above St. Louis. lat. N. 55.°

Minatarree

Ee-ah-chin-che-a (the Red Thunder) a celebrated
warrior, in war costume and equipments. Son of the vener-
-able chief, on the foregoing page, and heir apparent.

Minatarree

Bents-nau. (————) A young man, in a beautiful dress, not known to be celebrated otherwise than as a Beau.

Minatarree

Seet-see-be-a (the Mid-day Sun) An unmarried
girl, in a beautiful dress of mountain Sheep skins,
holding her Eagle tail fan in her hand.

Riccarree

Pa-too-ca-ra. (he who strikes) a favourite Warrior
of the chief, in War Costume — Shield, Bow & quiver
Slung .

A small tribe, of 15.00 on the W. bank
of the Missouri River, lat, N. 53°

Riccarree

Kut-sa-ra. (——————) A warrior in full dress, with his quiver slung on his back.

Riccarree

P'shan-shaw - (the sweet scented grass) an unmar -ried girl, in a beautiful dress, the tunique made of two mountain sheeps skins, and the Robe from the skin of a young Buffalo.

Riccarree

Stan=au=pat. (the Bloody hand) head Chief of the tribe, in a fine costume of skins, most beautifully garnished with porcupine quills, and fringed with scalp locks.

Rickarree

Ka_beck_a (the Twin) a Riccarree woman,
wife of the Chief, on the foregoing page.

Winnebago

Naw-kaw— (Wood) An aged man, head Chief of the tribe, with his War club on his arm.

At present a Small tribe, having been reduced by Small pox and Whiskey. residing on the Wisconsin, East of the Mississippi River. lat. N. 45°

Winnebago

Wah_chee_has_ka. (he who puts all out of doors)
a terrible Warrior, curiously dressed, with his
war club in his hand, and rattle snakes skins
attached to his arms.

Winnebago

Wa-con-chash-kaw. (he who comes on the thunder)
a young Warrior, with his War Club on his arm.

Winnebago

Hoo-wa-nee-kaw. (the Little Elk) a Celebrated Warrior, with his War club on his arm.

Mandan

Mah-to-toh-pa (the Four Bears) War chief of the Mandan tribe. one of the most celebrated chiefs known to have existed amongst the American tribes. in a very splendid costume, trimmed with Ermine and Scalp locks. His head dress, made of Ermine and War Eagles quills, descends to the ground, and is surmounted with horns, denoting his power, or authority as head War chief of the tribe.

A small tribe of 2.000. W. bank of Missouri, 2.000. miles above St. Louis. This tribe was almost entirely destroyed by Small pox the next year after the Author visited it.

Mandan

Mi-neek-e-sunk-te-cah (the Mink) the young (and favourite) wife of the War chief, on the foregoing page , in a beautiful dress of mountain Sheep Skins, and holding up to view, the Robe of her husband, with all the battles of his extraordinary life , painted on it .

Mandan

Ha-na-tah-nu-mauhk (the Wolf Chief) head civil chief of the Mandans, holding two calumets, (pipes of peace) in his hand: his dress, a very beautiful one, profusely ornamented with embroidery, and fringed with scalp locks.

Mandan

(———————) a Mandan Woman, wife and child of the Chief, on the foregoing page, in a fine dress.

Mandan

San-ja-ka-ko-ka. (the Deceiving Wolf) a noted
Warrior, with his shield on his arm, in a group
with two other young men, names not known.

These three portraits well illustrate the peculiar
mode of dressing and wearing the hair, prac-
-ticed by the Mandans. The hair of the young
men generally falls to the haunches or calves
of the legs, and is invariably divided into
flat slabs, and filled, in at intervals
of two or three inches, with glue and
red or yellow ochre.

Mandan.

Un-ka-ka-hon-she-kow. (the long finger nails)
a young Warrior, in War costume and equipments,
in the attitude of drawing his Bow.

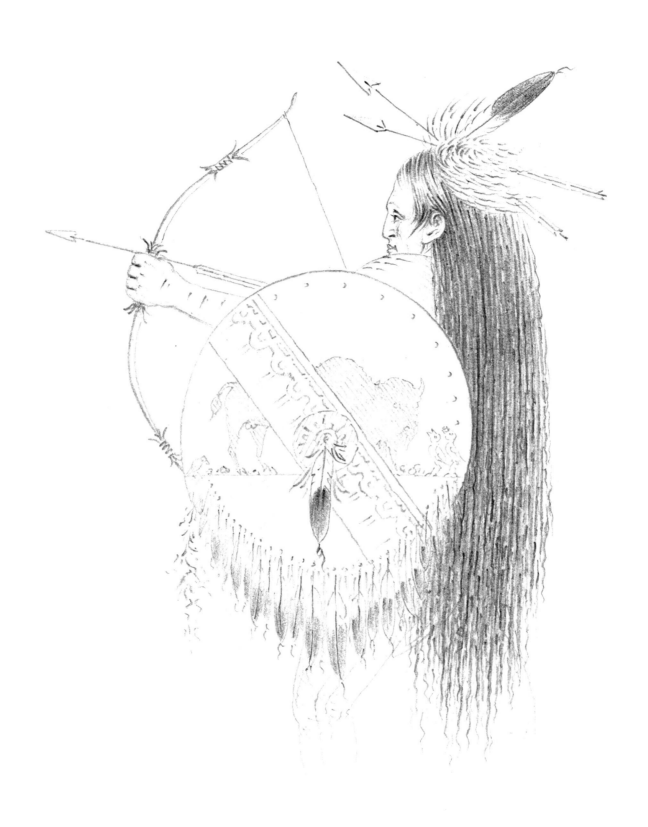

Mandan

Seek-hee-de (the mouse-coloured feather) a Young Warrior, in War Costume, resting on his lance.

Mandan

Mah-tahp-ta-ha (he who rushes through the middle)
a young Warrior in full War Costume, with shield
and quiver slung, and Scalping knife under his
belt; drawing his Bow.

Crow

Eeh-hee-a-duhks-chee-a (he who ties his hair before)
Chief of a Band, in a beautiful dress; his natural
hair descending to the ground

A tribe of 10.000. residing on the head waters
of the Yellow Stone River, at the base of, & in
the Rocky Mountains.   lat: N. 50°

Crow

Bi_eets_e_cure (the very sweet man) a Warrior of distinction, wearing a very beautiful Robe.

Crow

Pa-ris-ka-roo-pa (the two Crows) a celebrated
wise man and Counsellor, of the tribe.

Crow

Duhk-gits-o-oh-see (the Red Bear) a celebrated Warrior, wrapped in a beautiful Robe, with his pipe and tobacco Sac in his hands, and his body and his limbs curiously painted.

Crow

Chah－ee－chopes (—the Four Wolves） a famous Warrior; his natural hair, which reached to the ground, he is taking up in his hand, as he walks.

Crow

Ba-da-ah-chon-du (he who jumps over every one)
Chief of a Band, in a wonderful costume; Shield
and quiver slung. his lance in his hand, and his
head dress of War Eagles quills.

Crow

Ba - da - ah - chon - du (he who jumps over every one)
Same as on the foregoing page .

The portrait of this proud and vain man being finished,
he "took a good look at it", and declared himself very
well pleased with what he could see of himself; but
he was evidently disappointed and dejected, because
he could not see the hinder part of his beautiful
dress at the same time . The difficulty of doing
this in a portrait, was explained to him, and the
only way to remedy it, by making a second picture,
for which, he stood with great patience . and became
perfectly satisfied .

Crow.

Ha-chon-co-tah (————————————) a very distin-
-guished young Warrior, in full dress and equipments
for war, with Bow, Shield, and quiver, and necklace
of Grizly Bear's claws.

Crow

(——————) a Crow woman, wife of the young Warrior on the foregoing page, with her Eagle tail fan in her hand.

Crow

Pa-ris-ka-roo-pa. (the two Crows) head Chief of the tribe, in a beautiful dress, his natural hair reaching the ground, and his head dress made of the entire skin of a War Eagle.

Blackfoot

In-ne-o-cose. (the Buffalo's child) a Warrior of the Blackfoot tribe, in a fine dress. holding his lance and medicine bag, in his hand.

The most numerous and powerful tribe in N. Am. numbering 60.000. and occupying a vast tract of Country on the sources of the Missouri, and through the Rocky Mountains.

Blackfoot

Mix-ke-mote-skin-na. (the Iron horn) a famed Warrior, in full dress, wrapped in his Robe, with his panther skin quiver slung on his back, and his Bow & arrows clenched in his hand, under it, to be ready at a moments warning.

Blackfoot

Ah-kay-ee-pex-en (the woman who strikes many)
a Blackfoot woman, wife of the Warrior on the
foregoing page.

Blackfoot

Peh—to—pe—kiss (the Eagle Ribs) head war chief
of the tribe, in a splendid dress, profusely fringed
with scalp locks and Ermine; his head dress made
of Ermine & horns of the Buffalo.

Blackfoot

(——————) a Blackfoot woman, wife and child of the War chief, on the foregoing page

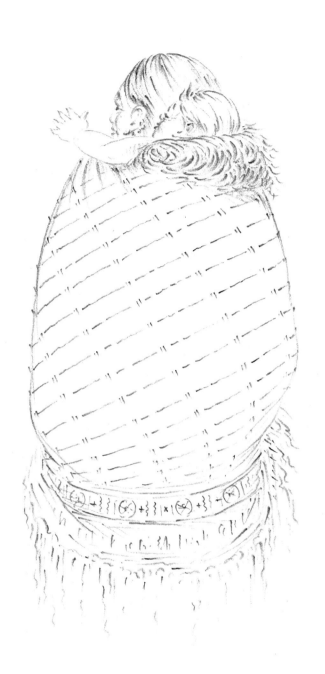

Blackfoot

Stu-mick-o-suks (the Buffalo's Backfat) head chief of the Blackfoot tribe, with a beautiful pipe in his hand, and in a costume of the most splendid and costly kind to be seen amongst the Am^n tribes, elaborately garnished with porcupine quill embroidery, and fringes of scalp locks.

132

Blackfoot

Ee-nis-kim, (the crystal stone) a Blackfoot woman, wife of the Chief, on the foregoing page, in a fine dress, with her Eagle tail fan in her hand.

Blackfoot

Wun-nes-tou, (the White Buffalo) the great medicine man and Counsellor of the chief, with his mystery drum and lance in his hands.

Saukie

Kee_o_kuk (the Running Fox) head chief of the tribe, one of the most celebrated and dignified chiefs on the U. States frontier. His Robe a red blanket, crossing his left shoulder, and a tomahawk, with scalp attached in his right hand, and his tobacco sac attached to his belt.

A warlike tribe of 6.000. residing until quite recently, in the State of Illinois, but now living W. of the Mississippi. lat. N. 44°

135

Saukie

(——————) a Saukie Woman, wife of the chief, on the foregoing page, in a costume chiefly made of civilized manufactures, And ornamented with a profusion of beads, buttons, & brooches.

saukie

Mee-sow-wauk (the deer's hair) a Saukie Boy
12. years old, son of the Chief, Kee-o-kuk, and
heir apparent.

Saukie

Pash-ee-pa-ho (the Little Stabbing Chief) An aged War chief of the Saukies, Curiously dressed, and holding his shield and War club in his hands.

Saukie

Ah-mou-a (the whale) a noted Warrior of the tribe, with Shield, war club & lance in his hands.

Saukie

Muk-a-tah-mish-o-ka-kaik (the Black Hawk)
War chief of the tribe, holding his fan made of the tail of
a Black Hawk, in his hand. A man whose name
has been rendered famous by a disastrous war which
got up, and waged for several years, on the U. States
frontier, and which resulted in the complete defeat,
and capture of himself, and most of his Warriors.

Saukie

Nah-se-us-kuk (-the whirling thunder) a distinguished Warrior, oldest son of Blackhawk, on the foregoing page, and taken prisoner with him, at the close of the Black Hawk War.

This tribe, it is seen, shave the head, like the Pawnees and Osages, and ornament it with the red Crest.

Saukie

Nah-pope (- the Soup) one of Black Hawks favourite Warriors, - taken prisoner with Back Hawk, and painted while prisoner of war, as seen by the Cannon Shot attached to his leg.

Saukie

Wah-pe-kee-suk. (the white cloud) a famous
Warrior, taken prisoner with the Black Hawk.

Saukie

Pash-ee-pa-ho (the Little Stabbing chief) (the younger) a desperate Warrior, whose name carried terror with it, over the whole frontier: like the four preceding ones, a prisoner of War, when painted, holding up a cannon that which was attached to his ancle.

K'nisteneux

Eeh-tow-ees-ka-zeet (he who has eyes behind him)
called "Bras cassé", from having his left arm broken &
disabled. The desperate feats of this celebrated young
man are almost beyond belief. He told the author,
while being painted, that he possessed six scalps
of his enemies, taken in battles which he had
fought with one hand!

K'nisteneux

Tsee-mount (a great wonder) a K'nisteneux woman, wife of the Warrior on the fore going page, in a pretty dress.

Pawnee pict

Sky-se-ro-ka. (————————) the leading Warrior of
the tribe, and a remarkeably fine man.

A Warlike, but not numerous tribe, on
the head waters of the Red River, near the
base of the Rocky Mountains, western
Texas.

Pawnee pict

Wee _tar_ra_sha_ro (——————) An aged and venerable chief — head chief of the tribe, with a beautiful pipe in his hand, and the numerous battles of his life painted on his Robe .

Pawnee pict

Kah—keet—se (the thighs) an unmarried
girl, her breast and arms curiously tattooed, a
custom but seldom practiced amongst the N. Am.
Indians.

Choctaw

Ha-tchoo-tuck-nee. (the snapping turtle) a young man, half caste, and educated.

A tribe of 6. or 8.000. recently removed from the State of Georgia to the upper Arkansas, W. of the Mississippi.

Choctaw

Mo-sho-la-tub-be (he who puts out and kills)
head chief of the tribe.

This tribe is chiefly civilized and agricul-
-tural.

Weeah

Go-to-kow-pah-a. (he who stands by himself) a
young man, said to be distinguished as a Warrior.
with his tomahawk in his hand.

Remnant of a tribe, State of Illinois

Weeah

wah—pon—je—a (the Swan) a fine looking
young man — not known to be distinguished.

Seminolee

Mic-e-no-pah (——————) head chief of the
Seminolee tribe, — a man very corpulent, an occur-
-rence exceedingly rare amongst the N. Am. Indians.

A numerous & warlike tribe, recently
removed from E. Florida, to the Arkansas,
700. miles W. of the Mississippi, by the
Gov't of the U. States, after a disastrous
war for several years.

Seminolee

How-e-da-hee (———————) a Seminolee woman, wife of the chief, on the foregoing page, with her infant, (pappoose) in her arms..

Seminolee

Os_ce_o_la (the Black Drink) a very celebrated warrior, half caste, who signalized himself, and took the lead in the Seminolee War.

Seminolee

Os_ce_o_la _. (the Black drink) a Boy 12. years old, Nephew of the Celebrated Warrior of the same name, on the foregoing page .

Seminolee

Ye-how-lo-gee- (the Cloud) one of the desperate
warriors who fought by the side of Osceola, in the Florida
War, and who was taken prisoner with Osceola, at the
close of that disastrous campaign.

Seminolee

Ee-mat-la. (King Phillipe) an aged chief
of the Seminolees, taken prisoner with Osceola &
the head Chief, and, like them, painted whilst
a prisoner of War.

Seminolee

La-shee (the Licker) . Called "Creek Billy", a celebrated Warrior of the Seminolees, seated on the ground, with his rifle in his hand.

Seminolee

Tin-ne. (——————) a Seminolee woman, wife of the Warrior on the foregoing page. with her infant in its cradle.

Arapaho

Hangs-kratch (Seafog) head chief of the tribe, wearing a Robe of the entire skin of a Grizzly Bear.

A small tribe in the Rocky Mountains, South of the great Salt Lake.

Arapaho

(————) an Arapaho Woman, wife and child
of the chief, on the foregoing page.

Arapaho.

Too-jen-ux-ta (the jumper) a famous hunter
And Warrior of the tribe.

Piankeshaw.

Men-son-se-a (the left hand) a celebrated
Warrior, with his War Club on his arm.

At present, a small remnant of a
Tribe, in Illinois. Civilized

Piankeshaw

(—————) a Piankeshaw Woman, wife of the Warrior, preceding page.

Piankeshw

Nee-a-co-mo (to fix with his foot) a young man not known to be distinguished.

Ottoe

Raw-no-way-wah-kra   (the loose pipe stem) Second chief of the tribe, in a fine dress. wearing a beautiful Robe, and a head dress of Eagles quills.

A Small remnant of a tribe. West bank of the Missouri, Lat. N. 44°.

Ottoe

(——————————) An Ottoe woman, wife of the chief on the foregoing page,

Ottoe

Wa-ro-nee-saw. (the Surrounder) head chief
of the tribe, in a curious dress, the tunique made
of the entire skin of a Grizzly Bear, with the
claws on — and another huge paw makes
his valued necklace.

Missouri

Haw-chee-ke-sug-a (the Osage killer) an aged man, and chief of the remnant of his once powerful tribe, now merged into the Pawnee tribe, and living under their protection.

Assinneboin

Wi–jun–jon (the Pigeons Egg head) a very
distinguished Warrior, and oldest Son of the Chief,
in a richly ornamented costume, the Shirt and
leggins fringed with Scalp locks.

A Warlike tribe of 8. or 10.000, living on the
head waters of Red River and the Assin-
-neboin, West of Lake Superiour,

Assinneboin

Chin-cha-pee (the fire Bug that creeps) glow-worm?) an Assinneboin woman, wife of the young warrior on the foregoing page, with her baton in her hand, with which the women of that tribe dig the "pomme blanche," a sort of wild turnip, called "wapsepinnican"

Assinneboin

(———————) An Assinneboin girl, unmarried,
daughter of Wi jun jon. (No 171)

Apachee

Be-las O-qua-na (———————) Called "Spanish Spur") the chief of a Band, said to have been very distinguished in his battles with the Mexicans.

A numerous and warlike tribe living in & West of the Rocky Mountains, on the northern borders of Sonora and Mexico.

Apachee

Nic-war-ra (the horse catcher) a celebrated Warrior, with his Bow in one hand and War club in the other.

Apachee

Nah_quat_se_o. (———————) a distinguished Warrior, in War plight, resting on his lance.

Apachee

Hu-tah (———) a terrible warrior, with quiver slung, and his bow and arrows in his hands.

Seneca

(—————————) Red Jacket, head chief of the tribe. This has been one of the most celebrated Indians on the U. States frontier during the last century. Eloquent in council and terrible in war. His name is closely identified with the early history of the U. States, as chief of the "Six Nations". The large silver medal on his neck, with the full length portraits in relief, of Gen'l Washington and the Chief shaking hands, was presented to him by the hands of Washington. For services he had rendered to the U. States army during the Revolutionary War.

This once powerful tribe, in the Western part of New York, is now reduced to a few hundreds.

Seneca

(——————) the Hard Hickory) one of the favourite Warriors of the Chief, with his pipe in his hand.

Seneca

(—————————) the Good Hunter) a celebrated
warrior, with his pipe tomahawk in his hand.

Ioway

Notch-ee-ning-a (no heart) head chief of the tribe, and a very celebrated man. with shield and lance, and necklace of the Grizly Bears claws.

At this time a small tribe, East bank of the Missouri, lat 44° N.

Ioway

Mu-hu-she-kaw. (the White Cloud) oldest son of the Chief on the foregoing page (at this time, chief of the tribe.

Ioway

Pah–ta–coo–chee. (the Shooting Cedar) a Brave
of distinction, with his War club on his arm.

Cherokee

Tol-lee (————) chief of a Band, civilized and half caste.

A tribe of 20.000. chiefly Civilized And agricultural. All removed by President Jackson, to the Arkansas, 700. miles W. of the Mississippi. They formerly lived in the State of Georgia.

Cherokee

Tuch-ee (————) called "Dutch", chief of a Band of Cherokees, a very distinguished man. This extraordinary man led 1500. of the wildest of his tribe a distance of 1200. miles West, abandoning their own Country and lands, to evade the en-crochments of Civilization, and there has main-tained his position against the constant assaults of the Osages, on whose hunting grounds he had located, and where he has remained for 12. years.

186

Kickapoo

Kee-an-e-kuk (the foremost man) Called the "Kickapoo Prophet", in the attitude of prayer, as he proposed. This tribe is semi civilized, and this man commenced preaching in his tribe a few years since, and ingeniously invented a short prayer which he carved in characters, on a maple stick, or baton, which he made it necessary for every member of his tribe to possess, and repeat, every morning and evening. He by this means abol-ished thee use of Rum & Whiskey in his tribe; and assuming the right of manufacturing and selling the batons, he in time amassed a little competency by his invention.

Kickapoo

Ah-ton-we-tuk (the Cock turkey) An aged man, who desired the Author to paint him saying his prayer from his baton.

Kickapoo

Ah-to-wat-o-mee. (———) a Kickapoo woman, reading her prayer from the maple stick, or baton.

Potowatomie

On-sau-kie (the Sac) a young man, reading his prayer from the maple baton.

The Kickapoo Prophet, having furnished all in his own tribe with his invented prayer, found it to his advantage to introduce it. And to Commence his preaching, in a neighbouring tribe, the Potowatomies, where he met with equal Success.

Potowatomie

Kee_se _ (———————) a Potowatomie woman repeating her prayer from the maple baton.

Potowatomie

Na-pow-sa. (the Bear travelling in the night) a noted Warrior, but represented without his Weapons or War Costume.

Iroquois

Not-a-way (——————) one of the chiefs
of the tribe, and said to have distinguished
himself as a warrior.

A small remnant of a once numerous &
warlike tribe — Lower Canada.

Iroquois

Chee‒a‒Ka‒chee (——————) An Iroquois woman,
Curiously mapped in her blanket.

Iroquois

Nox-to-ye (——————) a young Warrior, wrapped in his blanket, with his Bow and arrows clenched in his hand.

Kaskaskia

Kee-mon-saw. (the Little Chief) Chief of his tribe, now reduced to three persons — himself — his Mother, and his son, who is by his side.

Formerly a powerful tribe, on the W. of the Mississippi — lat. N. 41°

Kaskaskia

(————————) a Kaskaskia Woman, mother
of the young chief on the foregoing page.

Nayas.

Tsa-hau-mixen (the Rock that Slides down the hill)
a Secondary chief, but a man of great celebrity
amongst his people, wearing an oval block of wood
in the under lip, a peculiar & unaccountable cus-
-tom of that tribe.

A small tribe residing on Queen
Charlottes Island, and inlet, Pacific Coast,
lat. N. 52.°

Nayas

Kib-bee (the night bird) a young and unmarried girl, and daughter of the chief. on the foregoing page, also, with the block of wood in the underlip. And wearing a beautiful Robe or mantle, of their own manu-facture, Spun & woven, of the wool of the mountain Sheep, and wild dog's hair.

Nayas

Eeh-zep-ta-say-sa (——————) head chief of the tribe — an aged man, and said to have been distinguished as a warrior.

Nayas

Yen-ne-yen-ne (—————————) An unmarried girl, grand daughter of the chief on the foregoing page, wearing the block of wood in the under lip, and holding a canoe paddle on her arm.

Menomonie

Mah-kee-me-teuv (the Grizly Bear) Chief of the tribe, and a very distinguished man, his war club in one hand and a handsome pipe in the Other.

At present a small tribe, much reduced by small pox and whiskey. Western shore of Lake Michigan.

Menomonie

Chee-me-nah-na-quet. (the great cloud) Son
of the chief, on the foregoing page, and heir apparent,
with his war club on his arm.

Menomonie

Mee-cheet-e-neuh. (the wounded Bear's shoulder)
a Menomonie woman, wife of the Chief (No 201.)

Menomonie

Chesh-ko-tong (———————) a young Warrior of the tribe, with his War club in his hand; not known to have been distinguished.

Menomonie

wah_chees. (———————) a young man, with his war club on his arm, and blowing on his flute.

Peoria

Pah-me-cow-e-tah (the man who tracks) this elegant and amiable young man was chief of his tribe, and an advocate for temperance.

Small remnant of a tribe, State of Illinois.

Peoria

Kee-mo-ra-ni-a (——————) a young man, curiously dressed and painted, with his looking glass in his hand.

Peoria

(————————) a Peoria Woman, wife of the Chief, (No. 206)

Nez Percé

H'co-a-h'co-a-h'cotes-min. (no horns on his head)
a young Warrior, in a beautiful dress, with
his shield on his arm.

A small tribe, W. of the Rocky Mountains,
on the head waters of the Columbia R.

Nez-percé

Hee-ohks-te-kin (the Rabbit skin leggins) a
young Warrior, in a handsome dress, with a
scalping knife in his hand

Choctaw Ball player

Tul-lock-chish-ko (he who drinks the juice of the Stone)
The most famous Ball player of his tribe, in his Ball
play dress and paint, with his Ball sticks (or rackets)
in his hands. This tribe play with two rackets, one in
each hand, and make their tails of white horse hair.

Ojibbeway Ball player

Wee-chush-ta-doo-ta (the Red man) one of the most celebrated Ballplayers of his tribe. in Ball play dress and paint, and Ball stick or rackit, in his hands. This tribe use but one rackit, which they hold in both hands, and make their tails of Eagles quills.

Sioux Ball player.

Ah-no-je-nage. (he who stands on both sides)
This beautiful young man was said to be the most
distinguished Ball player in the Sioux tribe — in
Ball play dress and paint, and his racket in his
hands.

The game of Ball appears to be the favourite
game amongst all of the Am^n tribes, — In all
tribes, every player is obliged to observe certain
rules of dress, their limbs and bodies being
chiefly naked; and it is no uncommon
thing to see 4 or 5.00. of these beautiful &
graceful young men engaged in this
exciting game at the same time.

214

Assinneboin

Wi-jun-jon (the Pigeons Egg head) a celebrated young man, and son of the chief of the tribe, on his way to Washington , where he and the chiefs of several other of the remotest tribes had been invited by the President of the U. States, and where they were being conducted by Maj- Sanford, the Gov.t Indian Agent for those Tribes. This portrait was painted in Saint Louis, when the party were en route for Washington, and all in their beautiful and graceful, native Costumes

215

Assinneboin

Wi-jun-jon (the Pigeon's Egg Head) portrait of the same young man represented on the foregoing page, painted 18. months afterwards, on his way <u>back from Washington</u>, towards his native village in the wilder-ness, to which the author accompanied him and his Companions, a distance of 3.500. miles, and saw them enter their villages and meet their friends, and wives and children, in the costumes here represented, presented to them by the President of the U. States, their native dresses and equipments being left amongst the Indian Curiosities in the War department, at Washington.

Geo Catlin.

London. 1852.